SOLITUDE AND SOCIETY

NIKOLAI BERDYAEV

Solitude and Society

⊕

Translated by
George Reavey

Foreword by
Boris Jakim

SEMANTRON PRESS

Philmont NY

First Edition, Geoffrey Bles, Ltd., London, 1938
Second, enlarged edition © Semantron Press 2009
Semantron is an imprint of Sophia Perennis LLC
Foreword and Biography © Sophia Perennis 2009
Translated by George Reavey

For information, address:
Sophia Perennis, P.O. Box 931
Philmont NY 12565

Library of Congress Cataloging-in-Publication Data

Berdyaev, Nikolai, 1874–1948.
[IA i mir obektov. English]
Solitude and society / Nikolai Berdyaev;
2nd, enl. ed.

p. cm.
ISBN 978 1 59731 255 4 (pbk: alk. paper)
ISBN 978 1 59731 189 2 (hbk: alk. paper)

1. Solitude. 2. Knowledge, Theory of. 3. Personality.
4. Sociology. I. Title.
B4238.B43123 2009
197—dc22   2009022494

Cover design: Michael Schrauzer

CONTENTS

Foreword i

FIRST MEDITATION

THE PHILOSOPHER'S TRAGIC SITUATION AND THE PROBLEMS OF PHILOSOPHY

CHAPTER I. Philosophy Between Religion and Science: The Conflict of Philosophy and Religion: Philosophy and Society 3

CHAPTER II. Personal and Impersonal, Subjective and Objective Philosophy: Anthropologism and Philosophy: Philosophy and Life 19

SECOND MEDITATION

THE SUBJECT AND OBJECTIFICATION

CHAPTER I. The Knowing Subject and Man 27

CHAPTER II. The Existential Subject and Objective Processes: Knowledge and Being: The Subjective Revelation of Existence: Objective Processes and the Problem of the Irrational 35

CHAPTER III. Knowledge and Freedom: Intellectual Activity and the Creative Essence of Knowledge: Active and Passive Knowledge: Theoretical and Practical Knowledge 52

CHAPTER IV. The Degrees of Intellectual Community: The Extinction of the World of Things and Objects and the Approach to the Enigma of Existence 58

THIRD MEDITATION

THE EGO, SOLITUDE AND SOCIETY

CHAPTER I. The Ego and Solitude: Solitude and Sociability 65

CHAPTER II. The Ego, the Thou, the We and the It: the Ego and the Object: Communication between Consciousnesses 79

CHAPTER III. Solitude and Knowledge: Transcendence: Knowledge and Communion: Solitude and Sexuality: Solitude and Religion 86

FOURTH MEDITATION

THE EVIL OF TIME. CHANGE AND ETERNITY

CHAPTER I. The Paradox of Time: Its Dual Significance: The Non-Existence of the Past: The Transfiguration of Time: Time and Anxiety: Time and Creative Activity 97

CHAPTER II. Time and Knowledge: Remembrance: Time, Movement and Change: The Acceleration of Time and Technology 106

CHAPTER III. Time and Destiny: Time, Freedom and Determinism: Time and Finality: Time and Infinity 111

FIFTH MEDITATION

THE PERSONALITY, SOCIETY AND COMMUNION

CHAPTER I. The Ego and the Personality: The Individual and the Personality: The Personality and the Thing: The Personality and the Object 121

CHAPTER II. The Personality and the General: The Personality and the Species: The Personality and the Supra-Personal: Monism and Pluralism: The One and the Multiple 130

CHAPTER III. The Personality and Society: The Personality and the Mass: The Personality and Social Aristocratism: Social Personalism: The Personality and Communion: Communication and Communion 136

CHAPTER IV. The Personality and Change: The Personality and Love: The Personality and Death: The Old and the New Man: Conclusions 146

A Brief Overview of Nikolai Berdyaev's Life and Works 153

Bibliography of Nikolai Berdyaev's Books in English Translation (in alphabetical order) 160

FOREWORD

The title of the original Russian edition of this work is "I and the World of Objects" (*Ia i mir ob'ektov*, 1934). As the title of this work implies, Nikolai[1] Berdyaev tells us that man's "I," his consciousness, is thrust up against a world of impersonal objects (the "objectified" world) and thus finds itself in a condition of alienation and isolation. In five ontological and epistemological meditations Berdyaev clarifies this condition of "objectification"[2] and suggests ways it can be overcome, based on his "personalistic," "existential" philosophy. In other words, he examines how philosophy can serve to counteract objectification and human isolation.

For Berdyaev the philosopher's situation in the world is a truly tragic one. It is tragic in the face of the almost universal hostility directed against him: both religion and science are his avowed enemies. Especially acute is the antagonism between philosophy and religion, inasmuch as the latter claims to possess, in theology, a cognitive expression, a field of knowledge. In the conflict between religion and philosophy, truth is on the side of religion when philosophy claims to replace it in the sphere of salvation and eternal life; but truth is on the side of philosophy when it attempts to attain a higher degree of knowledge than that attained by the elements of naïve knowledge incorporated in religion. "In this sense," as Berdyaev says, "philosophy can help to purify religion by protecting it against the objective and natural processes assailing religious truths" (p. 15, present volume).

---

1. "Nikolai" is the more correct form of Berdyaev's first name. The original translations of Berdyaev's works into English used "Nicolas"; in order to avoid confusion this spelling is retained on the cover and title page.

2. Berdyaev develops his theory of objectification at length in his book *The Beginning and the End.*

According to Berdyaev there are two types of philosophy: one that affirms the primacy of being over freedom and one that affirms the primacy of freedom over being. In his own philosophy, Berdyaev affirms the primacy of freedom over being, and because of this his philosophy is a tragic one: "Tragedy springs from the impossibility of attaining being in an objective way, or of realizing communion between men considered as social beings; it springs from the everlasting conflict between the 'I' and the object; and, finally, it arises from the epistemological problem of solitude which is the special province of philosophy" (p. 18, present work). This affirmation of the primacy of freedom over being is connected with what Berdyaev calls his "personalist" philosophy. He asserts that the personalistic, subjective approach to philosophy is the only one likely to elicit a revelation of the original truth contained in primitive being; objective or impersonal investigation only succeeds in revealing the secondary and reflected aspects of being. Beyond the ontological domain, Berdyaev's personalism extends to the domain of social relationships. He writes that "every personalist philosophy helps to overcome human isolation by means of knowledge, and thus to transcend the immediate frontiers of individuality" (p. 24, present volume).

What, for Berdyaev, is the role of knowledge in his personalistic or existential philosophy? In this philosophy, the knowing subject apprehends not objects, not the objectified world, but receives a revelation of human existence and, through it, of the divine world. This revelation is the result of spiritual activity, of the integral reason which includes the life of the spirit rather than just employing rationalistic concepts. To apprehend existence is to illuminate it and to make it significant, to illuminate Being, and consequently to regenerate it and to enrich it with hitherto undiscerned elements.

Berdyaev goes on to explore the social content of knowledge, the intellectual ties that unite human beings and make their mutual comprehension possible. He affirms that knowledge

[ii]

enables man to escape from his self-confinement; it helps him overcome the disintegration resulting from the spatial and temporal division of the world. The degree of communication attainable by knowledge is largely dependent on the degree of community existing among people; Berdyaev asserts that the conditions of our degraded and disintegrated world tend to make the maximum social objectification the basis of universal communication. How does one overcome this predicament? One way is to integrate the social aspects of knowledge and to lay the foundations of a sociological philosophy. For Berdyaev, social being "can be truly illuminated only by existential philosophy, when envisaged in the light of the existential subject. Thus the objective world, the solid and inert world of matter, will dissolve into nothing when confronted with the revelation of the mystery of existence, with the spiritual, extra-natural revelation animating both the depths and the heights of being" (p. 61, present volume).

The third meditation is devoted to the "I," solitude, and society. For Berdyaev, the problem of solitude throws a great deal of light on the "I." "The failure of the 'I' to establish a relation with the 'We', and the acute and anguished solitude resulting therefrom, gives birth to the personality's growing consciousness of itself" (p. 68, present volume). The sense of solitude springs from man's endeavor to develop his personality regardless of the life of the species. "Only when man is alone, when he is overwhelmed by a distressing sense of his isolation, does he become aware of his personality, of his originality, of his singularity and uniqueness, of his distinctness from everyone and everything else" (pp. 68–69, present volume). In the extreme, case, he feels himself to be a stranger, an alien without a spiritual home. But man longs to escape from his solitary confinement, to enter into authentic relationships with other selves, with "Thou," with "We." How does he do this? How does he break through the shell of objectification and establish true communion with "Thou," with "We"? He does this by finding

[iii]

a reality deeper and higher than himself: "From the ontological standpoint, solitude implies a longing for God as the subject, as the Thou. The divine agency is the only one capable of enabling man to surmount his solitude, of making him aware of a sense of familiarity and relationship, and of disclosing a purpose commensurate with his existence" (p. 72, present volume).

In the final meditation Berdyaev explores the personality, society, and the communion of human beings. For Berdyaev the fundamental problem of existential philosophy is that of the personality; and conversely the personality is the principal category of existential knowledge. But what is personality? What is a person? The personality is a spiritual category; it is the spirit manifesting itself in nature. The personality is the symbol of human integrity, of permanent values, of a constant and unique form created in the midst of incessant flux. The personality is eternal and unique, but, paradoxically, it also permanently undergoes a process of creative change because it has need of time to realize its potentialities to the fullest. Personality should not be confused with mere individuality; the person is the human image who has realized to some significant degree his divine likeness. Personality breaks the spell of objectification, of the disintegration of the social community, and only persons can enter into true communion. Communion involves the reciprocal participation or interpenetration of persons. "This participation must take place in the very heart of the I's union with the Thou. The interpenetration of the I and the Thou is consummated in God. Communion involves the antitheses of the one and the multiple, of the particular and the universal" (pp. 141–142, present volume).

The exploration and realization of man as a person and of the communion of persons (of I and Thou in We) is the only thing that will lead to the rediscovery of man in his essential nature; and the rediscovery of man will lead to the rediscovery of God. For Berdyaev, this is the essential theme of Christianity;

the philosophy of human existence is a divine-human (thean-dric)[1] philosophy. Here is the conclusion Berdyaev comes to: "Truth is the supreme criterion of human existence. But truth is not an objective state, nor can it be apprehended like an object. Truth implies man's spiritual activity. Its apprehension depends on the degree of community between men, on their communion in the spirit" (p. 152, present volume).

BORIS JAKIM
2009

1. The doctrine of Divine Humanity, rooted in the Incarnation, involves the creative collaboration of man and God.

[v]

FIRST MEDITATION

THE PHILOSOPHER'S TRAGIC SITUATION
AND THE PROBLEMS OF PHILOSOPHY

CHAPTER I

PHILOSOPHY BETWEEN RELIGION AND SCIENCE—
THE CONFLICT OF PHILOSOPHY AND RELIGION—
PHILOSOPHY AND SOCIETY

The philosopher's situation is truly tragic in face of the almost universal hostility directed against him. This hostility has manifested itself in various ways throughout the history of civilization. Philosophy is, indeed, the most vulnerable part of culture; even its initial premise is incessantly questioned; and every philosopher has, first of all, to justify the validity of his claim to exercise his function. Philosophy is the victim of heterogeneous attacks: both religion and science are its avowed enemies. In short, it has never enjoyed the least semblance of popular support; nor does the philosopher ever create the impression that he is satisfying any 'social demand'.

In his theory of the three stages of human development, Auguste Comte assigns to philosophy the middle stage wherein metaphysics helps to bridge the gulf between religion and science. Comte was a philosopher himself, even though he did call his philosophy 'positivist', that is, scientific. He maintained that this scientific philosophy was a prelude to a purely scientific era as the next stage in the development of the human spirit. It was the essence of Positivism to reject the priority and the autonomy of philosophical knowledge, and to subordinate it ultimately to science. This idea of Comte's has become more firmly rooted in the general consciousness than would appear to be the case when we consider his Positivist doctrine in the narrow sense of the word. The term 'philosopher' had become popular during the Age of Enlightenment, but this vulgarization had merely degraded philosophy without producing a single great philosopher.

Religion was the source of the first and most violent attack on philosophy. The battle between these two is still being waged today, for, despite Auguste Comte, religion persists as an eternal

[3]

function of the human spirit. It is this conflict above all which gives rise to the philosopher's tragic situation: the debate between philosophy and science is much less virulent. The antagonism between philosophy and religion is especially acute because religion claims to possess in theology a cognitive expression, a field of knowledge. The problems posed and resolved by philosophy are invariably the same as those propounded by theology. But theologians have always tended to oppress philosophers; they have often persecuted them and sometimes have even had them burned at the stake. That this persecution was not a peculiar feature of the Christian world is proved by the treatment meted out to philosophers by the Arab theologians.[1] There are, moreover, the famous examples of Socrates condemned to drink hemlock, of Giordano Bruno burned at the stake, of Descartes forced to seek refuge in Holland, of Spinoza excluded from the synagogue. These examples will suffice to show what tortures and persecutions have been inflicted on philosophers by the official representatives of religion.

The philosophers' only means of defence was to expose the two aspects of the truth they were expounding. The reason for these tortures and persecutions must not be sought in the essence of religion, but rather in the fact that religion tends to objectify itself in the social structure. Revelation, which is the basis of religion, is not itself opposed to knowledge. On the contrary, there is a correspondence between them: revelation is what is *revealed to me* and knowledge is what *I discover myself.* How could there be any conflict between what I discover cognitively and what is demonstrated to me by religion? But actually this conflict can take place and put the philosopher in a tragic dilemma, for, as a believer, he may be prepared to accept revelation. We must rather seek the explanation in the complex nature of religion as a social phenomenon, in the fact that Divine Revelation, which is the pure and original essence of religion, becomes adulterated by the immediate reactions of the human community in which it takes place, and by the way in which men make use of it to further their own interests. This fact enables us to consider religion from the sociological standpoint.[2]

[1] Cf. *Gazali*, by the Baron Carra de Vaux.

[2] In Marx and Durkheim there are many sociological observations which are equally applicable to religion.

There is no essential affinity between revelation and knowledge, since the former contains no cognitive element. It only becomes a part of knowledge by virtue of what man contributes to it, by virtue of his thought; for theology, as well as philosophy, are purely human acts of knowledge. The intellectual interpretation of revealed truth is the expression not so much of the individual intelligence as of the organized collective, which is invariably the source of orthodoxy. Hence the conflict between philosophy and theology, between individual and collective thought. Revelation may therefore prove to be of capital importance to knowledge, for it constitutes a distinct philosophical experience, a transcendent event which philosophy can transform into an immanent datum. Spiritual knowledge is the essence of philosophical knowledge; the philosopher's intuition is therefore experimental.

Every theology comprehends a philosophy sanctioned by the religious community. This is especially true of Christian theology as expounded by the Doctors of the Church. Oriental patristic thought was impregnated with Platonism; in fact, it could not have built up the Christian dogma without the formal basis of Greek philosophy. Western Scholasticism was penetrated by Aristotelian philosophy, without whose categories, and notably the distinction between substance and accident, it would have been unable to define the Catholic doctrine of the Eucharist. Laberthonnière has said with some justification that medieval philosophy was not so much a servant of theology as theology was a servant of philosophy, that is, of a particular philosophy. That was the case of Saint Thomas Aquinas, who strictly subordinated theology to Aristotelian philosophy.

Hence the complex relations that have always existed between philosophy and theology. On the one hand, the doctrine of free philosophical speculation clashed with the dogmatism of determinist philosophy. In this way, philosophy became its own enemy, the victim of its own rigidity. On the other hand, the development of science was impeded by the immixture of all that was falsely scientific in the Bible—of its astronomical, geological, biological, historical teachings, which were mostly based upon the prejudices of a primitive society. The purely religious revelation contained in the Bible could not have proved such an obstacle. But religious revelation may be purged of those parasitical, philosophical or scientific elements,

[5]

which are the cause of incessant conflicts. The tragedy implicit in the philosopher's position is thereby diminished, but the philosopher himself is not eliminated. Philosophy, not satisfied to assign to itself religious ends, now puts forward religious claims. The aim of the great philosophers has always been to regenerate the soul through knowledge, and they have tended to regard philosophy as a means of salvation. This was true of the Hindoo philosophers as well as of Socrates and Plato, of the Stoics and Plotinus, of Spinoza, Fichte, and Hegel, and more recently of Vladimir Solovyev. Plotinus was hostile to religion because it required a mediator to effect salvation, whereas, according to him, philosophical wisdom was capable of achieving salvation without a mediator. Thus, there has always subsisted not only dissimilarity, but also conflict, between the 'God of the philosophers' and the 'God of Abraham, Isaac and Jacob'. The extreme form of this opposition is to be found in Hegel, who gave precedence to philosophy over religion in the process of spiritual development. The tradition of philosophy has been to contest popular beliefs—the myths inherent in religion and man's unquestioned submission to the authority of the past. Socrates perished a victim of this struggle. But although philosophy may start out by discrediting the myth, it ends by acknowledging it as the sum of philosophical knowledge. Plato demonstrated this fact when he passed on from *concept* to *myth* as the means of attaining true knowledge. Hegelian philosophy shows the same process at work in German Idealism.

We can trace the origin of this antagonism back to Hellenic civilization. For whereas the Greek religious consciousness subordinated life to destiny, their philosophy subordinated life to reason.[1] But Hellenic philosophy, in acquiring its universal importance, also laid the foundation of European humanism. We must not therefore expect philosophy ever to renounce its right to consider and, if possible, to resolve the essential problems of religion which theology claims as its monopoly. Prophecy has always been an adjunct of philosophy, and there is some justification in the proposed division of philosophy into the scientific and prophetic kinds.[2] It is the

[1] In his book, *Le Progrès de la Conscience dans la Philosophie Occidentale* (Paris, Alcan, 1927), L. Brunschvicg has given an excellent definition of the fundamental idea underlying Greek philosophy.

[2] Jaspers, *Psychologie der Weltanschauungen*.

[6]

prophetic type of philosophy which finds itself in perpetual conflict with religion and theology. The true philosopher is not only satisfied to apprehend the world; he also desires to modify, to improve, and to regenerate it. How could it be otherwise, since philosophy is essentially concerned with the purpose of our existence, of our destiny? The philosopher has always claimed not only to be inspired by the love of wisdom, but to be the expounder of wisdom itself; so that to renounce wisdom would be to renounce philosophy itself.[1] It is true that philosophy is primarily knowledge, but it is a *totalitarian* knowledge, one that comprehends all the aspects of human existence. Its essential aim is to discover ways of realizing *Meaning*. Philosophers have sometimes been content to expound a crude empiricism or materialism. But the essential character of a true philosopher is the love of the extra-natural; in this sphere he grapples with the transcendental world and refuses to reconcile himself to any interpretation of knowledge which would restrict his activities to the inferior world. It is the aim of philosophy to investigate beyond the limits of the empirical universe, and thus to penetrate into the intelligible universe, into the transcendental world. And I am very much inclined to believe that our love of metaphysics is engendered by our discontent with the world around us and our disgust at the empirical life.

The philosopher's immersion in the depths of existence, his Being, precedes, and also comprehends, his cognitive activity. The philosopher cannot build in the void; the pursuit of philosophy cannot separate or alienate him from Being, since he can only deduce knowledge from Being. The philosopher's tragedy is enacted in the depths of his own existence. Only his original participation in the mystery of Being can enable him to apprehend Being. But is not religion man's revealed life, his life in the depths of Being? How then can philosophy afford to ignore it? That is the essence of the tragedy as it affects the philosopher. On the one hand, he is incapable of supporting, must, indeed, refuse to suffer, the authority of religion; on the other, he tends to lose all notion of Being, and the strength it imparts, as soon as he becomes detached from religious experience.

Philosophical revivals always have a religious source. The pre-Socratic doctrines were intimately connected with Greek religious

[1] Husserl, *Philosophie als strenge Wissenschaft* (Logos, t. I).

[7]

life, and there was a close relationship between Platonism and the Orphic mysteries. Medieval philosophy was consciously Christian. The philosophies of Descartes, Spinoza, Leibnitz, Berkeley, as well as German Idealism, were founded on religious elements. I am even inclined to believe, however paradoxical it may sound, that modern philosophy as a whole, and German philosophy in particular, are by reason of their themes, and by the nature of their speculation, more essentially Christian than medieval Scholasticism, which was still Hellenic, Platonic and Aristotelian, in the principles of its reflection. Christianity had not yet entirely succeeded in permeating medieval thought.

With the dawn of modern times, which coincided with the birth of Cartesian philosophy, Christianity permeated the very essence of thought, and discovered a new aspect of the philosophical problem by setting up man as the centre of the universe in conformity with the revolutionary change brought about by Christianity. The pre-occupation with the *object* had been the fundamental tendency of Greek philosophy. But modern philosophy is concerned with the *subject*: that is the result of the emancipating influence of Christianity in liberating man from the power of the objective and natural world. The problem of freedom, which had played no part in Greek thought, was the direct outcome of this emancipation. I obviously do not mean to imply that the German philosophers were better Christians than Saint Thomas Aquinas and the Scholastics, or that their philosophy is wholly Christian. It need hardly be said that Saint Thomas was nearer the divine than Kant, Fichte, Schelling, or Hegel. But whereas the philosophical aspect of Thomism could have been elaborated in a non-Christian world, German Idealism is inconceivable outside Christianity. The effect of Christianity, as it penetrated more intimately into the core of thought and knowledge, was to free man from the inward authority of the Church and its theological restrictions. Philosophy acquired an increasing measure of freedom by stripping Christianity of its determinist philosophical elements. But the theologians steadily refused to acknowledge this emancipation of the Christian consciousness, the fact that Christianity has become immanent. This immanence has always been a subject of anxiety to the official Church. But philosophy, like true religion, may exercise a beneficial influence by purifying religion of its ex-

[8]

traneous and non-revealed elements, of all purely social accessories and outworn forms of knowledge.

The philosopher's heroic struggle was to be made all the more difficult by the appearance of another enemy. Indeed, the world seems to be united in denying to the philosopher the right to speculate freely. Hardly had he shaken off the shackles of religious dogma, of theology and of ecclesiastical authority, when he was expected to subscribe to the dogmas of science. Hardly had he become emancipated from the dictates of a superior power, when he was subjected to those of an inferior one. Thus hampered by both religious and scientific dogma, he found himself in a position of unbearable constraint. The philosopher has been allowed only the briefest intervals of free speculation, but these intervals have been fruitful in the highest philosophical achievements. The philosopher's position is never secure; he can never be sure of his independence; he is constantly the object of resentment. Even the University will only admit him on condition that he keeps discreetly silent about his own philosophy and devotes his attention primarily to the history of philosophy and the doctrines of other philosophers.

Science is as jealous of philosophy as religion. Like religion, science has built up a doctrine by which it claims to replace philosophy. This dogmatic scientific attitude is, indeed, the principal source of the attacks directed against it. Science has not only progressively reduced the competence of philosophy, but it has also attempted to suppress it altogether and to replace it by its own claim to universality. This process is generally known as 'scientism'. Max Scheller defined it as a revolt of slaves, the revolt of the inferior against the superior.[1] Indeed, why should one refuse to submit to religion if one is content to submit to science? It is Scheller's opinion that had philosophy submitted to faith, it would have dominated science. By faith, of course, he does not mean theology, the Church's exterior authority, religion become a social institution; for faith cannot enslave philosophy, it can only nourish it. But in its fight against authoritarian religion, which punished its daring researches by the stake, philosophy was led to repudiate faith as the inner light of knowledge.

These are the conditions which have conspired to make the philosopher's situation tragic. But, perhaps, the tragedy is inherent

[1] Max Scheller, *Vom Ewigen im Menschen.*

in the situation whether the philosopher is a believer or not. If the philosopher is a non-believer, his experience and horizon grow very narrow, his consciousness is shut off from all worlds but his own immediate one, his knowledge becomes impoverished, he imposes his own limitations upon Being. *The absence of tragedy is the tragic fact about the philosopher without a faith.* Whereas faith is synonymous with the consciousness of other worlds, of the significance of Being, a philosopher of this type tends to become the slave of his own freedom. When, on the other hand, the philosopher is a believer, the tragedy assumes another form. In his endeavour to exercise freely his cognitive activity, he comes into conflict with the social structure wherein faith is externalized, that is, with the authority of the ecclesiastical hierarchy and that of the theologians, who reinforce their restrictions with accusations of heresy and with persecution. This antagonism illustrates the perennial conflict between faith as a primary phenomenon, as a relationship with God, on the one hand, and faith as a secondary, purely social phenomenon, as a relationship with the religious community, on the other. But this is not yet the whole extent of the tragedy. The philosopher only experiences its full intensity when he is alone and isolated from his fellow-beings. The philosopher is unable to forget his faith or its revealed truth even when exercising freely his cognitive faculties. Here we are no longer concerned with the outward problem of his relationship with other men or the official representatives of religion, but with the inner problem of his knowledge in relation to his particular faith and spiritual experience.

Saint Thomas Aquinas solved this problem by establishing a hierarchical order in which each degree was both relatively independent and at the same time subordinate to the degree above it.[1] Thus philosophy functioned independently of faith; in fact, the Christian philosopher apprehended in exactly the same way as Aristotle. But in this hierarchy of degree, theology dominated philosophy as the supreme arbiter of all ultimate questions. In this hierarchy the degree of mystic knowledge had an even higher place than theology. Thus Thomism was able successfully to suppress any element of tragedy by carefully eliminating any antithesis between philosophy and faith.

[1] Cf. Jacques Maritain, *The Degrees of Knowledge* (Geoffrey Bles). This book is the last word on modern Thomism.

To all appearance philosophy was independent; but in reality it was completely servile, since it merely represented the dogmatic affirmation of a particular philosophy. Saint Bonaventura, on the other hand, resolved the problem in a different way: he affirmed that faith illuminated and transformed the intellect.[1] I am personally more inclined to agree with him despite the fact that he too had no inkling of the tragedy underlying philosophy.

It is an error to think that emotion can only be subjective, whereas thought is objective; that the knowing subject can only apprehend Being intellectually, whereas emotion confines him to the subjective world. Indeed, that is the conception of Thomism and of rationalist philosophy in general, that of almost all the Greek philosophers who endeavoured to pass from the δόξα to the ἐπιστήμη, from opinion to science, in fact, that of the majority of philosophers. It is based upon an old philosophical prejudice which we are only just beginning to discard to-day. Max Scheller and the other exponents of Existential philosophy have contributed a great deal to this end. Indeed, the very contrary is true. Human emotion is not subjective except for a small individual residuum; it is for the most part socially objectified. And inversely, intellection may be very subjective, and often even more individual and less dependent on social objectification than emotion, although this is only partially true. Moreover, the very meaning assigned to the terms 'subjective' and 'objective' is in need of being drastically revised. It is a question of the utmost importance to determine whether the apprehension of truth is subjective or objective. Whatever the solution, we can be certain of one thing: that philosophical apprehension is a spiritual act which involves not only intellection, but also the concentration of the totality of man's spiritual forces, of both his voluntary and sentient being.

The present tendency is increasingly to admit the existence of an affective mode of apprehension as it had been imagined by Pascal, and as it has been affirmed in our day by Max Scheller and Keyserling.[2] It is a prejudice to believe that knowledge is always rational, that there is no such thing as irrational knowledge. Actually, we apprehend a great deal more through feeling than by intellection; and it is a matter of some note, that not only love and sympathy,

[1] Gilson, *La Philosophie de Saint Bonaventure.*
[2] Keyserling, *Meditations Sud-Americaines.*

[11]

but also hostility and hate, may help to further our knowledge. The heart is the centre of the entire man. That is above all a Christian truth. The whole appreciative aspect of knowledge is affective, for it expresses the 'reasons of the heart'. Criteria of value have an important place in philosophical knowledge. Since there is no way of apprehending *Meaning* without a criterion of value, its apprehension is primarily based on the knowledge of the heart. Philosophical apprehension involves man's entire being, that is, the union of faith and knowledge. An element of faith is present in all philosophical speculation however rational; it was present in the inspiration of Descartes, Spinoza and Hegel.

This is one of the facts which demonstrates the inconsistency of the idea of a 'scientific philosophy'. This philosophy is the invention of thinkers devoid of any true philosophical gift or vocation, of those who had nothing to contribute to philosophy. The product of a democratic century which discredited the very idea of philosophy, 'Scientism' is not even in a position to appreciate the significance of science itself, of man's intellectual potentialities, since the very fact of propounding the problem transcends the frontiers of science. Scientism treats everything, even the subject himself, as object.

The existence of philosophy presupposes an appropriate *philosophical* mode of cognition as distinct from a *scientific* one. A 'scientific' philosophy is the negation of essential philosophy, the denial of its primacy.[1] To admit an effective mode of apprehension, a sensible apprehension of value, is not to deny reason. On the contrary, reason itself demands the restitution of its integrity as it was understood in the Middle Ages, when, despite the intellectualism of the Scholastics, the intellect was often assigned a spiritual significance. The task of philosophy is not to invalidate reason, but to discover its contradictions and to demonstrate its limitations while preserving its immanence. In this light, Kant's doctrine of the antinomies retains its validity. We must not seek the criteria of truth in reason or the intellect, but rather in the integral spirit. The heart and the conscience remain the supreme agents of value as well as of knowledge. Philosophy is not synonymous with science; it is not even the science of

[1] Husserl is not an exponent of 'scientism', for he interprets 'science' as did the Greeks, and not in the sense assigned to it by the nineteenth and twentieth centuries.

essences; its function is to endow the spirit with a creative consciousness of the meaning of human existence. This supposes in the philosopher an inherent experience of human contradictions and of the tragedy implicit in his vocation. How could any philosopher fail to find his knowledge both impoverished and diminished if he persisted in remaining unconscious of this tragedy?

Intuition is the *sine qua non* of philosophy. Every true philosopher has an original intuition of his own. Philosophical intuition cannot be deduced from anything else; it is primary, and secretes in itself the light which will illuminate every act of knowledge. Neither religious nor scientific truths are adequate substitutes for intuition. Philosophical knowledge depends on the range of experience, and it also supposes an essentially tragic experience of all the contradictions of human existence. *Philosophy is therefore based upon the maximum experience of human existence.* This experience integrates man's intellectual, affective and volitional life. Reason is independent of all external authority, is outwardly autonomous; it is not, however, inwardly independent in relation to the whole life of the philosopher engaged in the pursuit of knowledge. It will not allow itself to be stripped of its feelings and volition, of its loves and hates, of its criteria of value. It discovers its ontological foundation in the depths of its own Being, in the intimacy of its own existence; it adapts itself to the philosopher's belief or scepticism; it varies with his belief as the consciousness expands or contracts. But revelation transforms it.

We may note here that the doctrine of the catholicity of reason is erroneous.[1] That *a priori* are mobile and mutable. We must avoid confusing the Divine Revelation and the world of invisible things with their intellectual apprehension. This latter is a human attribute; it is man who apprehends the Divine Revelation and the invisible world. But the Divine Revelation changes man's reason, which becomes inwardly transformed as a result of the shock of the revelation, and man is thus enabled to perceive clearly all its inherent contradictions and limitations. The mere acceptance of revelation is a philosophical act however elementary. Revelation provides realities and data of a mystic order; but the intellectual attitude adopted towards these realities and data has nothing to do with

[1] Scientific theorists like Meyerson insist on the universality of reason: cf. *De l'Explication dans les Sciences.*

[13]

revelation, since it is itself based on some definite philosophy. No man can live without any basis of philosophy, however primitive, naïve, childish or unconscious. Every man thinks and speaks, makes use of notions, categories, symbols, myths, and gives vent to appreciations. There is always a childish philosophy at the foundation of a childish faith. Thus the uncritical acceptance of Biblical science, that of primitive mankind, involves the use of certain categories of thought such as 'Creation', for example, envisaged as a moment in time.

Intellection is an act and not a passive reception of things; it endows the object with meaning, and establishes a similitude, a common measure between the knowing subject and the known object. That is especially true of theosophy. Knowledge, indeed, is *humanization* in the deepest ontological sense of the word. There are various degrees of humanization: the highest lies in religious knowledge. For man is the image and likeness of God; and consequently God contains in Himself the image and likeness of man, the pure essence of humanity. Next to it is the degree of philosophical knowledge, which also involves humanization, that is, the apprehension by man of the mystery of Being inherent in him, the apprehension of the meaning of existence in so far as it is commensurable with human existence and destiny. Humanization is at its lowest degree in scientific knowledge and particularly in the physico-mathematical sciences.[1] Contemporary physics demonstrate the dehumanization of science, for their researches are leading them outside the human universe as understood by man. But physicists are blind to the fact that the very researches of dehumanized physics symbolize the power of human knowledge; and that their rapid progress only serves to demonstrate man's originality when confronted with the mysteries of nature, and above all his essential humanity. All knowledge is rooted in the depths of human existence and manifests man's efficacy as an integral being whose power extends to contradictions and conflicts, to the very heart of the tragedy inherent in the philosopher's situation.

Knowledge is based upon the action of three principles: the human, the divine and the natural. It is the outcome of the reciprocal action of human culture, Divine Grace, and natural necessity. The philosopher's tragedy has its origin in the attempt to restrict his pursuit of knowledge by the invocation of Divine Grace or by an

[1] Léon Brunschvicg discovers spirituality in the mathematical sciences.

appeal to the universal character of natural necessity. If God and nature are the objects of philosophical investigation, then its antagonism to both dogmatic religion and science is inevitable. But its true sphere is the investigation of human existence, human destiny and human purpose. Man is the real subject of the philosopher's knowledge; through man he can apprehend both God and nature; but he cannot pursue his investigations without stumbling against objectified forms of knowledge which claim to expound the ultimate truth concerning God and nature. The philosopher is ready to accept Divine Revelation and faith, but he must avoid endorsing their naturalist interpretation, just as he must refuse to accept the universalist claims put forward by natural science.

In the conflict between religion and philosophy, truth is on the side of religion when philosophy claims to replace it in the sphere of salvation and eternal life; but truth is on the side of philosophy when it claims to attain a higher degree of knowledge than that attained by the elements of naïve knowledge incorporated in religion. In this sense, indeed, philosophy can help to purify religion by protecting it against the objective and natural processes assailing religious truths. The living God to Whom men address their prayers is the God of Abraham, Isaac and Jacob, not the philosophers' God, the idea of the Absolute. But the problem is even more complex than Pascal imagined, for the God of Abraham, Isaac and Jacob was not only the God Who Is, the living and personal God, but also the God of a primitive nomad tribe, a God reduced to the intellectual and social level of that tribe. The spirit in its quest of knowledge is always bound to clash with the slumbering spirit of tradition. It is not easy for philosophy to adapt itself to the gregarious spirit. Philosophers have always been a small group of men among the mass of mankind. Is it not surprising then that such a small group of men should have been the object of so much hostility? Allied against them we find religious men, theologians, the clergy and the faithful, scientists and specialists of all kinds, politicians and social organizers, statesmen, conservatives and revolutionaries, engineers and technicians, artists, and, finally, the mass of mankind. Thus it would seem that philosophers are the most negligible members of the State and society, those who have no important function to perform in either political or economic life. And yet the ruling classes or those who solicit power, those who play as well as those who aspire to play some part in the life of the State and of society, are invariably hostile to philosophers; they seem unable to forgive philosophy for not serving their ends, for being the unjustified preoccupation of only a few men, a vain play of the intellect. But is philosophy any of these things? It is, indeed, difficult to understand why the indulgence of a few men in a pastime apparently devoid of any reality or reason should excite so much ill-will and almost universal disapproval.

There is a complex psychological problem at the foundation of this. If it is true that philosophy is alien to the majority of men, it is also true that every man, unknown to himself, is in a certain sense a philosopher. Those who have but a vague idea of the technical apparatus of philosophy do not hesitate to employ the term as an expression of derision or reproach. In common speech the word 'metaphysics' is almost a term of abuse. The metaphysician has become a comic character. He may happen to be one; but it is nevertheless true that every man, whether consciously or not, does attempt to resolve questions of a metaphysical nature which are essentially more familiar to him than the problems of mathematics and physics. A current philosophy is as common a feature of various social groups, classes or professions, as politics. The man who feels an aversion to philosophy, or who despises philosophers, has yet a private philosophy of his own. If this were not true of the statesman, the revolutionary, the specialist, the engineer and the technician, they would not think the philosopher superfluous.

Experience teaches us that the philosopher's position, and indeed, that of philosophy itself, is most precarious. Not only does the philosopher not fulfil any social function, but the dignity of his calling elevates him above the duties prescribed by society. Philosophy is essentially a personal rather than a social function. Whereas both religion and science, though so different by nature and often hostile to one another, are socially protected and, by reason of their social rôle, enjoy the support of interested communities, philosophy is defenceless and alone. No one will take up arms in defence of the philosopher who generally even lacks economic support. The truth he discovers takes no account of other people's reasoning; it is his own reason that must furnish the revelation of the supra-human and the divine. Society does not aid him in his pursuit of knowledge. In every philosopher there is always something of Spinoza and his destiny. The philosopher's social insecurity, the personal character of his thought, and his general situation, all combine to make his vocation akin to the prophet's. The prophet's position is even more precarious; he is more liable to be persecuted when he preoccupies himself with the destinies of a people or a community. Thus the prophetic type of philosopher is the most disarmed, the least tolerated, and the most solitary. When the philosopher does adhere to a tradition, he is conscious of himself as a member of a philosophical family, as a member, say, of the Platonic or the Kantian schools. A philosophical tradition may even crystallize itself on the basis of a national culture or it may lead to the foundation of a school, and in these ways the philosopher may find some support and protection against attacks. That does not apply, however, to philosophical intuition at its birth, in the creative act in the precise meaning of the term. Academic philosophy, for example, is a social institution benefiting by the means of protection at the disposal of society. But the founders of religions, the prophets, the apostles, the saints, the mystics, are all equally unable to defend themselves against society. Thus religion is granted social recognition and protection only when it transforms itself into a social institution.

Man has a choice of two attitudes in every creative and intellectual act: he can confront the mystery of Being, the Divine mystery; or he can restrict his relationships to a purely social plane. In the first case, he attains to an authentic philosophy by means of intuition and revelation; in the second, he is forced to adapt his philosophical knowledge as well as his revealed truth to the needs of a particular society. But in return for social security thus granted, he has to falsify his conscience and help to propagate socially useful falsehoods. In society, in the company of other men, man tends to become an actor; he is one also when he becomes an author. He is obliged to play a part because of his social position; like an actor, he depends on other people, on the public, and on the police to protect him in case of need. The man who sets out in quest of truth, and who finds himself face to face with the Divine mystery, not only often cries in the wilderness, but also leaves himself open to attack by the pontiffs of both religion and science. This situation is implicit in the very nature of philosophy and constitutes its inherent tragedy.

The different types of philosophy may be variously classified, but one distinction at least would appear to be corroborated by the history of philosophy. That is the duality underlying the fundamental principles of philosophy, a duality which intervenes effectively in the solution of all important problems. The choice between these two types of philosophical approach is apparently not dictated by any external authority; so that the choice once made, attests to the personalist character of philosophy. These two types may be analysed by confronting the opposing theses:

1. The primacy of freedom over Being; the primacy of Being over freedom;
2. The primacy of the subjective over the objective world; the primacy of the objective over the subjective world;
3. Dualism; monism;
4. Voluntarism; intellectualism;
5. Dynamism; statism;
6. Activism; and the sense of creation; passivity; contemplation;
7. Personalism; impersonalism;
8. Anthropologism; cosmologism;
9. Spiritual philosophy; naturalism.

These principles may be variously combined to form different systems. I, personally, have made my choice: I have resolutely chosen the first series of theses which maintain the primacy of freedom over Being. The admission of a fundamental opposition between freedom and necessity, spirit and nature, subject and object, personality and society, the individual and the general, postulates a tragic philosophy. To affirm the primacy of Being over freedom is to eliminate tragedy; to affirm the primacy of freedom over Being is to postulate it. Tragedy springs from the impossibility of attaining Being in an objective way, or of realizing communion between men considered as social beings; it springs from the everlasting conflict between the Ego and the object; and, finally, it arises from the gnosiological problem of solitude which is the special province of philosophy. That is, indeed, the problem with which this book is chiefly concerned. It has also a bearing on the distinction between a multi-plane and a uni-plane philosophy.

PERSONAL AND IMPERSONAL, SUBJECTIVE AND OBJECTIVE PHILOSOPHY—ANTHROPOLOGISM AND PHILOSOPHY—PHILOSOPHY AND LIFE

Kierkegaard lays particular emphasis on the subjective and personal character of every philosophy, on the living presence of
the philosopher in the act of speculation. By his opposition to Hegel,
by his revolt against the exponents of universal and objective reason
and against the philosophy of general concepts, he often reminds us
of Bielinsky,[1] whose influence is perceptible in the dialectic of Dostoievsky's Ivan Karamazov. Kierkegaard is, of course, a more genuine philosopher than Dostoievsky. But to return to our main argument: Can philosophy be anything but personal and subjective?
I shall discuss this question in detail later; in the meantime, I shall
attempt to draw an important distinction between truth and objectivity. Philosophy cannot help being personal even when it aspires
to be objective. Every true philosophy bears the stamp of its author's
personality. This is true not only of very individual philosophers like
Saint Augustine, Pascal, Kierkegaard, Schopenhauer and Nietzsche,
but also of philosophers like Plato, Plotinus, Spinoza, Fichte and
Hegel. The imprint of a philosopher's personality is already manifest
in the choice of problems and in a predilection for one or other of
the philosophical types we have defined, as well as in the nature of
the philosopher's predominant intuitions, in the amount of attention he apportions to particular problems, and in the degree of his
spiritual experience.

The fact that the Ego is the foundation of all philosophy does not
mean that it is circumscribed by the systems it engenders. True
philosophy is not content to investigate the object, but grapples with
its underlying reality in the anxious hope of probing the meaning of

[1] Consult the very interesting work, *Le Socialisme de Bielínsky*, edited by
Sakouline, and containing Bielinsky's letters to Botkine.

life and of personal destiny. Even Spinoza's geometrical and objective philosophical system[1] demonstrates that philosophy springs out of the philosopher's reflection on his destiny. This fact cannot be stressed sufficiently often. The faculty of apprehension is essentially that of the Ego, of man as a concrete being, as a personality, and not that of the universal spirit or of the universal reason, of the impersonal subject or of the general consciousness. Thus the fundamental problem of philosophy is that of human knowledge, of man's own personal knowledge. Every creative thought is essentially personal, but that does not imply that its individual author is an egoist, just as the distribution of light may vary even though it emanate from a unique source.

We must be sceptical of the philosophers' claim that their thought is exempt from all affectivity. Ultimately, the most objective and impersonal of them all apprehend through feeling. There can be no doubt that Descartes arrived at his *cogito* through an emotional experience, that he must have made his discovery in an ecstasy of an emotional kind.[2] The fact that he exercised his intellect to achieve this result is no evidence of its exclusive use; for, at that particular moment, his powers of reflection were coloured with intense emotion. Spinoza's *Ethics* are permeated with feeling despite the geometrical method employed therein; and his *Amor Dei Intellectualis* likewise betrays a violent emotivity. Thus 'Intellectualism' may be founded on personal emotion, while 'objectivity' may be nothing more than a term to conceal human passion. In this sense, Hegel's philosophy is no less subjective than Nietzsche's. Accordingly, any strictly 'objective and impersonal' philosophy is almost certainly devoid of any creative originality.

The subjective approach is the only one likely to elicit a revelation of the original truth contained in primitive Being; objective or impersonal investigation only succeeds in revealing the secondary and reflected aspects of Being. Needless to say, an artificially induced originality only makes its real want the more conspicuous. We must deliberately discard the prejudice, that personal and subjective modes of thought restrict the individual and make it impossible for him to affirm his place in the universe or to commune with the divine world.

[1] Cf. L. Brunschvicg, *Spinoza et ses contemporains* (Paris, Alcan).
[2] Cf. J. Maritain, *Le Songe de Descartes.*

The very contrary is true: objective and impersonal modes of thought are the greatest obstacle to the individual's emergence from his self-confinement and to his communion with the universe. It would be a mistake to confound the personal mode of apprehension with ego-centricity, which is a form of perpetual self-imprisonment leading eventually to insanity. Egocentricity is, indeed, the Original Sin. The personality, on the other hand, is the reflection of the divine image and likeness, and, as such, it is the true path leading to God. The personality is, indeed, the primary subject of philosophical speculation. This latter is empirical only in so far as it depends on the range and plenitude of the philosopher's experience. The personality is the image of the living and integral man, who thinks in terms of personal and human philosophy. This man is inseparable from philosophy, since the philosopher, as the subject of knowledge, is immersed in Being; his existence precedes his apprehension of Being, and this fact determines the quality of his knowledge. He apprehends Being because he is himself a part of Being.

A philosopher's vision is invariably limited; the plenitude of Being and total illumination are denied to him; and this accounts for the divergences between the various philosophical currents. His vision of the original Light is limited by his immediate perception, by the few beams that penetrate the dark recesses of his consciousness. Beyond this meagre revelation he has no alternative but to refashion accepted ideas and to rely on knowledge gleaned from study. At the back of every philosophy lies the torturing desire to realize life, its meaning and destiny. Thus philosophy is primarily the doctrine of man, the doctrine of integral man elaborated by integral man. But this doctrine is the exclusive province of philosophy, and not of biology, psychology, or sociology. It is impossible to abstract philosophy from anthropocentrism and anthropologism. In their anxiety to eliminate the Original Sin of egocentricity, which alone invalidates anthropocentrism, many philosophers have attempted this task. It is equally true that all the attempts to eliminate the philosopher considered as a man, and also as the fundamental theme of humanity, have proved chimerical and illusory. The ambiguous position of anthropocentrism is due to the fact that, although man, as the image and likeness of the Higher Power, of the divine essence of Being, is the key to the enigma of Being, he is restricted to a particular theme and, as a result, inclined to reduce all Being, however divine, to the level of his own imperfection. Instead of attempting to eliminate all trace of anthropocentrism from philosophy, we should endeavour to purify and exalt this anthropocentrism so as to enable the philosopher to reflect the image of the Higher Being inherent in him. Philosophy cannot be autonomous, if by that we mean abstracted from the vital experience of the integral man, or independent of the knowing subject immersed in Being. Indeed, it could not claim autonomy without blinding itself to reality. Philosophy must therefore be anthropological, since its knowledge of Being is derived from man. Its chief problem is to purify man's anthropological nature, so as to reveal his *essential* nature, the *transcendental* man, whom we must be careful not to identify with the non-human 'transcendental consciousness'.

Philosophy is also anthropological in the sense that it cannot be abstracted from life or be made purely theoretical. It is essentially active, and has a useful function to fulfil in ameliorating life, as the great philosophers, the lovers of true wisdom, have always endeavoured to do. The drudgery, ugliness and injustices of everyday life tend, on the one hand, to make man seek refuge in another world, the world of metaphysical or mystic contemplation, the world of ideas or the City of God; and, on the other, to excite his creative activity to transform the everyday world and build it up into something new. True philosophy cannot be derivative because it is founded upon wisdom. Mere abstraction makes the philosopher's position false and untenable. Just as the philosopher's language must have something in common with colloquial speech, so philosophy must grow out of experience. It is, after all, a vital function, an integral expression of spiritual life. How could it claim to apprehend the mystery of Being, if it refused to explore human destiny or to show sympathy for its unhappy lot? Philosophy is essentially a vital act. Abstract reasoning is the fault of those metaphysicians of the past who have ignorantly sacrificed their interest in life, mankind and the world and have taken refuge in an ideal citadel of concepts. In these circumstances, it is hardly surprising that the metaphysician tended to become an object of curiosity and derision, a symbol of ignorance rather than of wisdom. Actually, the only true basis of metaphysics is to be found in the knowledge of life, of concrete reality, of man and the human destiny. Metaphysics should be the expression of a living movement, in which the philosopher must himself actively participate.

Karl Marx, who claimed to be a disciple of the German Idealists, Fichte and Hegel, propounded the idea that philosophy could no longer content itself with a mere knowledge of the world, but should also endeavour to transform and recreate it. He maintained that Fichte's theoretical and abstract thought should be given a practical expression. The marxists, and especially the communists, have since distorted this idea in a monstrous fashion by illogically giving it a materialist foundation—that is, a foundation of passive philosophy. There is, of course, a considerable element of truth in the Marxian idea. It can, however, be expressed in a different form, and notably, as in Feodorov's *Projective Philosophy* which likewise propounds an active transformation of the world. Are we to conclude then that the function of philosophy is purely 'social'? Surely not, for in that case philosophy would be a passive thing. It is not the privilege of society to dictate to philosophy, but that of philosophy to dictate to society. The development of philosophy from Hegelianism to Feuerbach's Anthropologism is significant as indicating an inevitable passage from a philosophy of universal and general concepts to one of human spirituality. Feuerbach's materialistic deviation has helped to obscure this truth, for materialist philosophy is incapable of conceiving man as an integral and concrete being. But obviously the development of philosophy could not be finally resolved in that mysterious drama—the concept of Hegelian dialectic.

The Greeks maintained that philosophy was primarily concerned with the general as opposed to the particular and the individual. Thus Hellenic philosophy set out to discover the world of Ideas situated beyond the sensible mobile world of multiple experience. It never departed from this fundamental premise; and, as a result, it failed to distinguish the individual or to discover the personality and the importance of the idea of freedom. Scholastic philosophy inherited this restricted outlook, with the result that its sphere of speculation was circumscribed by the premise of the universal concept. These limitations are still present in a lesser degree in the modern Nominalist philosophies. But the experience of Christianity, and

[23]

above all of the Revelation, have opened entirely new perspectives —those of the mystery of the personality and of freedom.

Personalist philosophy, as I understand it, has nothing in common with the *subjectivist, individualist, empirical* or *nominalist* currents of to-day. The 'general' category, which is usually opposed to the individual and the particular categories, is a false one and should be discarded forthwith. As we shall discover hereafter when investigating the problem of the personality in relation to society, the 'general' category has no ontological validity. The universal principle itself is not a 'general', but an individual one. Thus God is universal, but not general; He is also individual. The 'general' principle is a compromise, an error, which has reached the stage of *apophatic* knowledge—of knowledge in the process of discarding all notions and determinations, all finality. Its extra-personal and extra-individual sphere is that of the objective social world which is far removed from authentic reality, from the existential and the divine world. It is primarily social, the product of sociological elaboration. The 'general' principle excludes the human or the philosophical element. There is no more important task then for Personalist philosophy than to discover the authentic reality behind the superficial semblance of the 'general'. Spinoza was certainly not inspired by any 'general' idea when, in his *Amor Dei Intellectualis*, he endeavoured to transcend his solitude in a vision of Beatitude. Every Personalist philosophy helps to overcome human isolation by means of knowledge, and thus to transcend the immediate frontiers of the individuality.

SECOND MEDITATION

THE SUBJECT AND OBJECTIFICATION

CHAPTER I

THE KNOWING SUBJECT AND MAN

German Idealism dealt a blow to the objectivism of Greek and Scholastic philosophy from which it cannot hope to recover. It is a mistake to suppose that German Idealism, with Kant at its head, has invalidated the notion of Being itself. Its criticism was chiefly directed against the affirmation of naïve Realism, that the objective world and Absolute Being were in every respect identical. Descartes had already begun work in this sense, but pre-Kantian rationalism had not gone deeply enough into the problem. It had become imperative to transfer the centre of philosophical gravity from the *object* to the *subject*, and to seek a subjective solution of the problem of Being. The world of objective realities, of objects, was accordingly relegated to a secondary place, as the phenomenal world. And although Kant made the mistake of opposing the phenomenal world to the object itself as devoid of both experience and knowledge, he was nevertheless right in attempting to distinguish between them, for this distinction led to the discovery of the active subject.

Philosophical theory has always been based upon the opposition of subject and object.[1] But we have still to determine the nature of the subject. And we have also to elucidate the relationship between the pure subject of cognition, the *gnosiological* subject, and man the Ego, the knowing subject. German Idealism has replaced the problem of man as the concrete knowing subject by the problem of the pure subject—by Kant's transcendental consciousness, Fichte's non-individual and non-human Ego, Hegel's universal spirit. As a result, knowledge ceased to be a peculiarly human property and became, instead, a divine prerogative inherent in universal reason or the universal spirit. Thus man was no longer the knowing subject. The effect of this was to depersonalize philosophy. Personalist philosophy

---

[1] N. Hartmann, *Grundzüge einer Metaphysik der Erkenntnis*. Although he breaks away from Kantian Idealism, he still maintains the opposition of the subject and object.

was identified with psychologism, which, in its turn, was made accountable for the human personality, the human Ego and man. But the fundamental problem of the nature of man's relationship to his personality, on the one hand, and to the transcendental consciousness, universal reason and the gnosiological subject on the other, remained unsolved. For ultimately, there can be no denying the fact that man is the knowing subject. Kant employs *a priori* forms to remove the scepticism directed against his transcendental consciousness. But is the knowing subject any the further advanced as a result? How is the transcendental consciousness related to the individual human consciousness? How does it establish the validity of knowledge? Or again, to employ Idealist terminology, how is the logical related to the psychological?

This argument is fundamentally unsound because it interprets all human qualities, and human consciousness in particular, solely from the standpoint of psychology, thus abstracting it from the logical and transcendental spheres of consciousness. The result is to make man himself an obstacle to philosophical knowledge. This constitutes an attempt to eliminate man's 'subjective presence' from philosophy. In the same way, theologians have often claimed that man is an obstacle to Revelation, thus apparently overlooking the fact that Revelation takes place solely for man's benefit. Indeed, philosophy has always been unconsciously anthropological and anthropocentric; and although it may have been often hostile to psychologism, it cannot attack anthropology without endangering its own existence. Psychologism implies relativity. But human nature and its inherent possibilities of knowledge constitute the true philosophical problem. In avoiding this problem, German Idealism demonstrated its chief deficiency.

In avoiding this problem it illustrated its essential monism. I have more than once suggested, however paradoxical it may seem, that there must be some connection between German Idealism and Lutheranism. This conclusion needs to be explained more fully. What affinity can there be between Fichte and Hegel, on the one hand, and Luther on the other? At the first sight they would appear to be antipodal. Luther excommunicated reason, repudiated philosophy, and proclaimed human nature sinful and corrupt. Hegel, on the contrary, glorified reason, deified philosophy, and had a very feeble sense of sin. But spiritual influences work in a mysterious,

[28]

subterranean and surprising way. Luther ascribed everything to Grace and divine intervention, nothing to human action or human freedom.[1] He did not admit the reciprocal action of the divine and human natures. German Idealism has done little more than work out this monistic tendency. It has secularized Lutheran Grace, considered as the unique source of all goodness, by transferring its attributes to knowledge. Thus the transcendental consciousness, the universal reason and the universal spirit, are but the secular forms of Lutheran Grace, which had claimed to be the source of all knowledge. Hegelian philosophy in particular clearly affirms that the knowing subject is God Himself, His reason, His spirit, and not man. Thus the Grace that would originally have made philosophy superfluous has finally contributed to its glory and even apotheosis.

The difficulty here encountered is due to the *refusal to recognize the reciprocal action of man's two natures.* German Idealism endows the pure subject with the maximum of potentiality; it even attributes creative activity to it, thus considerably diminishing man's contribution to knowledge. A world thus engendered by the constructive activity of the intellect leaves hardly any room for the creative activity of the human consciousness. The contribution made by human freedom to intellection is not even considered. The activity of the gnosiological subject is exaggerated at the expense of human activity, which is represented as passive in the inmost depths of knowledge; man merely obeys the dictates of the transcendental consciousness. Although this tendency was not yet clearly implied in Kant, who was not an avowed monist, it does become evident in Fichte, the early Schelling, and finally Hegel.

These reflections bring us to the religious sources and foundations of philosophical theory. These are contained in the theandric idea, in the idea of the reciprocal action of the divine and human natures, of the freedom and creative power inherent in both these natures. The theandric idea is the basis of the very possibility of a Personalist philosophy, of any philosophy dealing with the human personality. It is true that the human consciousness tends to materialize itself, to become the merely passive reflection of its originally active nature. It is, however, capable of renewed activity once it has shaken off the fetters of the objective world. My use of the term 'object' will never

---

[1] Cf. Luther's masterly work, *De Servo Arbitrio.*

connote that any form of knowledge is independent of the subject;
it represents, rather, a particular way of apprehending knowledge
and Being. For me *objectivity* can never be synonymous with *truth*,
with an *independent attitude* towards *subjective states*; on the contrary,
the term will connote the dependence of objectivity on subjective
states, and on human relationships. In the same way, *objectification*
can never be identical with *manifestation, revelation* or *incarnation*.

The existential philosophies of Heidegger and Jaspers would appear to deal with the problem of man. Heidegger's ontological
approach, as expressed in his *Sein und Zeit*, is based on human existence. He situates man's 'anxiety' and fear, his subjection to the
commonplace, to the 'One' (*Das Man*), as well as death and the
decadent world, in the ontological rather than psychological sphere.
Similarly, Jaspers' 'limit-situation' (*die Grenzsituation*) has, like the
problem of communication between men, a metaphysical significance. And yet neither Heidegger nor Jaspers really considers the
problem of man; nor do they attempt to build up a consistent philosophical system on the basis of philosophical anthropology. They
have not worked out or elaborated the rich material inherent in their
systems into any definite philosophical doctrine of man. They leave
the problem of human nature unsolved. Nor do they attempt
to explain why the structure of Being is only revealed in human
existence and human destiny. They have no explanation to offer as
to the origin of the essentially human virtue of knowledge. Jaspers
differs from Heidegger in his disbelief in the possibility of an objective metaphysics or an objective ontology based upon a scientific
model; he regards metaphysics in a subjective and personal light, as
a system of symbols. He is, indeed, an extremely subtle psychologist.
But a subjective and Personalist defence of metaphysics should not
be undertaken in a sceptical spirit, but rather in the belief that it
leads to a higher knowledge. We thus come back to the fundamental
problem of man, which the philosophers have, for some strange
reason, never seriously considered. They have perhaps ignored it
because it has generally been regarded as the province of theology,
or, at least, of an essentially religious philosophy.

Brunschvicg[1] affords an interesting example of the attempt to

[1] Cf. *Spinoza et ses Contemporains. Les Étapes de la Pensée mathématique. Le
Progrès de la Conscience dans la Philosophie occidentale.*

eliminate anthroposophy from philosophy. His philosophy is based upon a type of mathematical idealism originally derived from Plato. Brunschvicg maintains that every philosophy of a biological tendency is anthropocentric, and that every mathematically inspired philosophy is absolutely disinterested and dehumanized. For this reason, he considers mathematical truths to be spiritually more important than the problem of the purpose of human existence. For Brunschvicg mathematical science is a degree of spirituality; and he would, therefore, have philosophy free itself ultimately from any vestige of the Christian myth of man and his centripetal situation in the universe. His conception has affinities with Spinozism, which attacked the cruder forms of anthropocentrism and anthropomorphism. It is true that the problem of man's centrality is above all a Christian problem, and that every anthropological philosophy is necessarily a Christian one. Greek philosophy, for example, did not pose the problem of man in all its plenitude; it only discerned reason in man without perceiving the fundamental and problematical implications of that discovery.

But man is immersed in the depths of Being. His existence precedes his awareness of himself; his potential knowledge depends upon his Being. His immersion in Being is precisely the quality which makes intellection possible, for transcendence is not *objective* or authoritarian, but immanent. We must affirm the primacy of integral man, of man rooted in the very heart of Being, as against the consciousness or the confrontation of subject and Being. We must not confuse integral man, whose real nature is reflected in the intimacy of his existence, with the psychological or sociological man, who is a part of the objective world. The natural world was rediscovered and rehabilitated at the time of the Renaissance, when man came to regard himself as part of nature. He did so in the belief that he would emancipate himself. But the time has now come to rediscover and rehabilitate man, *no longer envisaged as a fragment of nature and the objective world, but as a being in his own right, situated in the extra-objective and extra-natural world, in the very core of his own existence.* When this shall have been accomplished, the philosophical problem will no longer present itself as the opposition of subject and object, but as that of philosophy and Being.

In philosophical theory, the subject is usually opposed to, rather

[31]

than identified with, Being. But man, on the contrary, is a part of Being. He is an object and a slave of the natural world only in so far as his existence is objectified. But in his own depths he continues to be himself, to fulfil his destiny. It is only in this sense, in an onto-logical rather than subjective or psychological sense, that man is the subject of philosophy. The spirit, of course, can never be object, but only subject; it is, however, the subject in a deeper sense than is affirmed by gnosiology. Man is unable to apprehend the meaning of life objectively, since the object can have no meaning but that ascribed to it by the spiritual subject. All meaning is revealed within the Ego, within man; and it is commensurable with the Ego. When, on the other hand, meaning assumes some objective form, when it becomes an extrinsic datum posited by the natural world, then its character becomes predominantly social and symbolic of man's spiritual enslavement. Husserl maintains that the confrontation of existence with Being leads to the elucidation of truth; but he also affirms that knowledge is not a subjective sensation or spiritual re-flection, that Being reveals itself in the human consciousness. Thus the knowing subject is already himself synonymous with Being, and, as such, he confronts the world.

Kierkegaard, on the other hand, challenges most theoreticians by affirming the coexistence of truth and reality in a subjective state. He has every reason to affirm this, since the object can have no criterion of truth. Its only criterion is furnished by the intellectual and moral consciousness of the Ego. An objective criterion of truth could only be exercised by a collective consciousness, which only complicates the problem. Communication with truth invariably helps the Ego to escape from its self-confinement. *Knowledge attained is a symbol of victory over egocentricity.* It is not egocentric, but personal; egocentricity and egoism are the product not of the personality, but of the Ego. Our aim should be to sacrifice the Ego and to realize the personality. The passage from the human Ego to the divine world, which constitutes man's final triumph over the sin of egocentricity, may take place in communion with others, but not by their means; thus no person can claim to be the inspiration of another's attitude to God. If this were not true, man would occupy a merely sub-ordinate place on the plane of social objectification. Knowledge is primarily an act, and only secondarily a theoretical object; for the very idea of proposing knowledge as an object constitutes an intellectual act. The process of objectification involved in the middle phase of consciousness—a process subordinating consciousness itself —is in all circumstances a secondary manifestation. The primary reality and knowledge precede or succeed this objectification.

Philosophical theory has only transformed man into the subject in opposition to the object, the objective world, and the process of objectification. Considered on an extra-natural plane, independently of his opposition to objectified Being, the subject is man, a personality, a living being, existing in the heart of Being. The truth is inherent in the existing subject and not in the opposition of the abstracted subject with the object. The objective world has no criterion or source of truth. Intellectualist philosophies, whether Greek or Scholastic, tend to make the subject passive by endowing him uniquely with intellectual perception. As a result, we are in danger of identifying concepts with Being, of regarding the uninterrupted activity of intellection as a purely reflective activity. The human intellect was originally confronted with chaos; but since its function is to clarify and to illumine, to introduce meaning into a world devoid of any, the very act of apprehending the dark and meaningless world should bring illumination and significance.

Knowledge is essentially active because man is active. When philosophical theory is based on the opposition of intellection and Being, the affirmation that philosophy only reflects Being passively, and that it is wholly determined by Being as by a created world, is no longer tenable. Intellection is the outcome of free human activity; it is not merely reflection, but also creative transfiguration, which we must understand in a different way from Kant and Fichte. True, their subject, their transcendental consciousness, and their Ego do, in a sense, participate in the work of creating the world, but their creation is devoid of any element of human freedom or humanity. Man himself does not share in this subjective creation of the world by the exercise of any cognitive activity. In reality, the world thus created is not the work of the subject, but of God; this creation, however, is incomplete and requires man's active collaboration. His creative freedom should extend to all spheres and it should pursue its creative work in the sphere of knowledge itself. The human consciousness cannot apprehend the world passively; for apprehension involves concentration, imagination and intense awareness. This intensity must emanate from within rather than from without. This indicates that the subjectively conceived world is essentially a human conception, a world dependent upon man as a being, as a concrete existence, and that knowledge symbolizes the relationship between one being and another, a creative act in the inmost depths of Being. The perception of things varies with the point of view, with that of the subject or object, with that of the spirit or nature, with that of the personality or society. These different standpoints constitute so many different worlds; there exists no absolutely objective world, but only varying degrees of objectification.

The Absolute is situated in the non-objective, spiritual plane which precedes objectification, in the existential plane which the objectifying processes have not yet made part of the natural sphere. Man relies upon knowledge to defend him from the constraining aspects of a multiple world; he shuts out some of its aspects, admits others, and often despises or condemns those aspects which he fails to understand. In the process of intellection man is constantly transcending himself, for, as the subject, he is powerless to apprehend the plenitude of Being; and his knowledge suffers as a result by being invariably partial.

Man's inspiration towards plenitude is a creative incentive. His creative activity is even manifest in the process of objectification; for example, in the prodigious discoveries of mathematical science; but it is still more evident in the transcendence of the objective sphere, in the metaphysical exploration of the essential and the existential realms. But as Renouvier has very justly said, the human consciousness fails to be Absolute because its nature is relative. How then does man endow knowledge with an element of freedom? That is the problem we shall have to consider hereafter. It is the problem of knowledge, active or passive. Philosophical theory has so far been baffled by the enigma: *Why is the material and irrational object reflected in the immaterial and rational subject in the form of knowledge?* And indeed, no solution of this enigma can be forthcoming as long as *knowledge* is regarded as a mere subjective reflection of the object, and Being as an objective state from which the subject has been eliminated.

CHAPTER II

THE EXISTENTIAL SUBJECT AND OBJECTIVE PRO-
CESSES—KNOWLEDGE AND BEING—THE SUBJECTIVE
REVELATION OF EXISTENCE—OBJECTIVE PROCESSES
AND THE PROBLEM OF THE IRRATIONAL

When, in opposing the subject and the object, philosophical theory abstracts them both from Being, it makes the apprehension of Being impossible. To oppose knowledge and Being is to exclude knowledge from Being. Thus the knowing subject is confronted with Being as an apprehensible but abstract object with which no communion is possible. The objective state is itself the source of this abstraction, which excludes any communion or, as Levy-Bruhl puts it, any 'participation'[1] in the object, although concepts may be formed about it. The nature of the object is purely general; it contains no element of irreducible originality, which is the sign of the individual. That is, indeed, the essential distinction between the subject and the object.

Objective processes transform Being into a superstructure of the subject, elaborated for philosophical purposes. It is precisely because the subject identifies himself with this objective superstructure that he discovers therein a more suitable expression of his own cognitive structure. Abstraction is one definition of knowledge; but this abstraction is the work of the subject, of the knowing spirit itself. When he is abstracted from his inner existence, the philosophical subject loses all contact with Being, and his existence becomes dependent on the objective processes he has set in motion. Thus intellection no longer affects or inheres in Being; on the contrary, it becomes an absolutely extrinsic and logical rather than a spiritual act.

This is the tragedy of knowledge as expounded by German

[1] Cf. Levy-Bruhl, *Les Fonctions mentales dans les Sociétés inférieures*,

Idealism, which reaches its highest expression in the neo-Kantian school. True, the opposition of knowledge and Being, of the subject and Being, is part of an older philosophical tradition; but the manifest superiority of the German post-Kantian philosophies lay in their critical approach to the problem of objectification and in their recognition of the importance of the knowing subject. Pre-Kantian, and particularly Scholastic philosophy, had approached the problem realistically and had identified the concepts elaborated by the subject with Being itself. This was the origin of naturalist metaphysics with its doctrine of substance and its hierarchy of Being. In the light of these facts, the advent of Kant and of German Idealism marks a most important stage in the history of human self-consciousness. It was a step towards human emancipation, towards freeing man from the constraint and slavery of the objective world. The very fact of a critical awareness of the subject's participation in the objective processes, implied the subject's deliverance from the external tyranny of the objective world. The work done in this sphere by Kant, and the German Idealists who followed on Descartes and Berkeley, precludes any return to the ancient metaphysical system of the substantialist type which identified Being with object. Henceforth Being could only be apprehended subjectively, and the subject, accordingly, assumed an ontological character. Philosophers like Kant, Fichte Schelling and Hegel, have built up a metaphysical system on a subjective basis, but in the process they interpreted the subject in an objective and non-existential way. As a result, they have made no contribution to the problem of the human personality, but have tended rather to espouse the cause of universalism. They affirmed that the subject was neither human nor personal. Thus, after Kant and Fichte, Hegelian philosophy established itself on the whole, despite its irrational elements,[1] as a new type of objective rationalism. Actually, we can only transcend the tragic implications of Idealism by advancing in the direction of what is to-day called *Existenzphilosophie*, or Existential philosophy, rather than by reviving any of the pre-Kantian metaphysical systems.

Kierkegaard laid the foundations of Existential philosophy by challenging the Hegelian universal concept and its fatal effect on the individual. Kierkegaard's thought is not fundamentally new; it is

[1] Cf. Kroner, *Von Kant bis Hegel.*

very simple,[1] and is motivated by the sense of anguish to which the personal drama of his life gave rise.[2] His tragic experience led him to emphasize the existential character of the knowing subject, the initial fact of man's immersion in the mystery of existence. The philosophy most expressive of man's existential character is the most vital; for philosophers have too often tended to overlook the fact of their own existence as distinct from their power of intellection, and the fact that their philosophy is little more than the translation of their existence. We may therefore conclude, though not in Kierkegaard's own terms, that, from the existential standpoint, the philosopher is situated on the extra-natural plane, that is, in the inmost depth of Being; for the subject is himself a part of Being and, as such, communes with its mystery. Among the number of existential philosophers we may count Saint Augustine and Pascal, in a sense Schopenhauer and Feuerbach, Nietzsche and Dostoievsky. But Kirkegaard was the most significant exponent of this philosophy. In my book *The Philosophy of Freedom*, written some twenty years ago, I had already defined Existential philosophy, though I did not use that term, as a philosophy which *represents* something in itself, which is a manifestation of Being, of existence, as opposed to the type of philosophy which treats of something extraneous, of the objective world.

On the basis of this affirmation, which has some affinity to Jaspers' conception, Existential philosophy represents a mode of non-objective intellection. Ordinarily, the process of abstraction eliminates the mystery of existence, of concrete Being. There can be no worse aberration than to identify the object with reality. To know and to objectify or to abstract are currently regarded as synonyms. But the very opposite is true: effective knowledge involves familiarity, or, in other terms, a subjective approach, an identification of oneself with the subjective existence. It is our duty, therefore, to reject the naturalist, *objective* conception of Being in favour of the existential one. Even phenomenology may be interpreted as an experience transcending the objective state. Communion with men, animals, plants or minerals is an extra-natural phenomenon revealing potential ways of knowing.

[1] Cf. in particular, Kierkegaard's *Philosophische Brocken*.

[2] The same is true of Leon Shestov, whose philosophy consists in the self-negation of philosophy.

Heidegger and Jaspers are the two leading contemporary representatives of Existential philosophy. Heidegger distinguishes between *essential* existence and *objective* existence or the *Dasein*. The state of being-in-the-world, the *Dasein*, inspires anxiety and fear; it is above all a temporal state destined to become the One, *das Man*. The banality of everyday existence robs death of its tragic poignancy and obscures the fact that it is the direct outcome of the finite state, of the *Dasein*; but the sense of tragedy is intensified when the fact of existence is predominant. Existence is a state of Being, of which the *Dasein* is a part. *Seiende,* on the other hand, is essential Being, my own self, my own essential nature. The originality of Heidegger's philosophy lies in the importance he attaches to the *In-der-welt-sein,* the state of being-in-the-world, as one of the necessary but degraded aspects of Being. Human existence is substantial. Concrete existence has more importance for Being than essence. Thus philosophy should be concerned with existences rather than with essences. Heidegger's *Dasein* involves anxiety and fear of the degraded world as a constituent part of its ontological nature. Man's moral conscience requires him to experience this anxiety in a world where he is at the mercy of objectivity. The *Dasein* is a state of guilt, all that constitutes human anxiety and the oppressive sense of human insignificance.

In the light of Heidegger's philosophy, it is difficult to discover the genesis of the human conscience. His philosophy is anti-Platonic and anti-spiritual. Its pessimism makes it more purely a philosophy of 'being-in-the-world' rather than an Existential philosophy. To use Heidegger's own expression, his ontology is that of nothingness, of being-nothing. He makes no attempt to explain the nature of extra-temporal existence. But Heidegger does set out to establish an Existential philosophy; and the essential problems with which he is concerned, such as the banality of everyday life, degradation and death, are different from the problems usually treated by philosophy. These problems acquire a new importance in his philosophy, because he interprets them from the ontological rather than from the psychological standpoint.

The same problems are to be found in Jaspers,[1] with whom I have more in common than with Heidegger. The problem which pre-

[1] Karl Jaspers, 1st Bd. *Philosophische Weltorientierung*; 2nd Bd. *Existenzerhellung*.

occupies Jaspers most of all is that of man's 'limit-situation', that of the communication between one Ego and another. He is particularly careful to point out that the Ego, as an entity, is distinct from universal Being. The Ego can never be an object, because the object is never existential.[1] Jaspers is much clearer on this point than Heidegger. He demonstrates that the existential Ego, as opposed to the empirical Ego, can transcend temporal existence because its entity is extra-temporal. The idea of transcendence is of capital importance in Jaspers' philosophy, and it dominates his 'metaphysics', which he regards not as a science, but as a function of language intended to make intelligible the transcendence immanent in the existential consciousness. For this reason he considers it essential to be able to decipher the scripture of signs, and ascribes great importance to numbers and symbols.

Both Heidegger and Jaspers have undoubtedly made an original contribution to thought, even though their philosophies are extremely tragic and pessimistic because they lead man to the brink of an abyss. The trend of modern philosophy as manifest in Descartes and the Cartesians, in Kant and the neo-Kantians, and in the scientifically-minded Positivists, was essentially naturalist. Existential philosophy, however, advances a stage further. That is its great and unquestioned merit; but its originality has so far been limited by its associations with Kierkegaard, who affirms that existence is the primary concern of the existential subject.[2] What then, we may ask, is existence? It is, in the first place, a very different thing from intellection. As Bergson has demonstrated, it is situated in time, but not in space. It is dynamic as contrasted with the immobility of logic. To formulate an idea of himself the intellectual subject is forced to deny his existential nature, to face the antagonism between abstract thought and existence. Existence excludes the idea of mediation: to exist is to be an entity. The *particular* is more deeply rooted in Being than the *general*. The world of eternal Ideas is not the image of existence, as the Platonic tradition would have us believe; this image is more truly reflected in human nostalgia, despair, unrest and dissatisfaction. Thus contradiction is more fruitful than identity. *Ob-*

---

[1] Ideas of a similar nature may be found in Gabriel Marcel's *Journal Metaphysique*; cf. notably the appendix which treats of the problem of objectification.

[2] S. Kierkegaard, *Philosophische Brocken.*

jective thought conceals no mystery, but *subjective* thought does. Existence is synonymous with becoming. There may be a logical system behind it, but a system of existence is inconceivable. Objectively we treat of *things*, but subjectively our concern is with the *subject*; and even our preoccupation with objective truth is essentially *subjective*. This is, indeed, the very core of Kierkegaard's thought, which may be summed up as the *identification of the knowing subject with the existential subject:* the primary purpose of subjective thought is to manifest its existential nature. The essentially Christian character of Kierkegaard's 'paradox' represents a departure from immanentism. For Kierkegaard, man's inner life, his existence, has nothing immanent about it. He interprets 'phenomenon' to mean self-revelation, that is, transcendence. In this connection, we may recall the distinction established by N. Lossky between immanence in the consciousness and immanence in the conscious subject.

Despite a certain affinity between Kierkegaard's philosophy and that of Heidegger and Jaspers, there is yet an essential difference between them. For Kierkegaard, philosophy is itself existence rather than an *interpretation* of existence; whereas, for Heidegger and Jaspers, who are concerned with a particular philosophical tradition, philosophy is synonymous with interpretation. Their aim, especially Heidegger's, is to elaborate philosophical categories on an existential basis, to make categories of human anxiety or the fear of death. Heidegger's attempt to break away from the domination of rationalist and objective knowledge constitutes a very remarkable and in many ways original achievement. But actually, concepts and categories are only a means of apprehending the *Dasein*, the being-in-the-world, that is, objective or completely abstract Being. *The concept is only related to the object;* therefore, as Jaspers admits more clearly than Heidegger, the inner existence or primary Being can only be apprehended through the imagination, the symbol and the myth. The elaboration of concepts is an objective process leading inevitably to a hypostasis of the intellectual categories themselves. As a result, this type of philosophy is primarily concerned with essences, substances, objects; it makes God Himself an object, whereas a philosophy primarily concerned with the personality is able to apprehend existence. Thus Heidegger speaks with greater authority of the *Dasein* than of existence itself; in fact, although he considers the objective state a degraded one, his own philosophical approach contributes to maintain the world in its degraded state.

Existential philosophy cannot be based on concepts and ordinary categories even when it is ontological. *The concept is invariably concerned with something, it is never that something:* it is never existential. Vladimir Solovyev established an interesting distinction between abstract Being as the *predicate* and concrete Being as the *subject*. The notion *is*, is an example of abstract Being; the notion *I am,* is an example of concrete Being. Unfortunately, this distinction[1] is often ignored, and the predicates are converted into hypostases. In his criticism of German Idealism, Vladimir Solovyev would appear to have penetrated into the very heart of concrete Being. And yet his philosophy cannot really be called Existèntial, because it is still dominated by rationalist metaphysics; his most genuine expression lies in poetry rather than in philosophy. A judgment of existence is not simply a judgment of what exists; it is also a judgment made by the existing subject. Existence is not deduced from, but precedes judgment; and logical Being is the product of intellection, of an objective process.

For this reason, Husserl's Phenomenology fails to be an Existential philosophy, although it exercised a considerable influence on Heidegger. Husserl affirms that real objects are inherent in the essences and need no mediation; he also contends that evidence is not a state of consciousness, but the presence of the object itself. Phenomenology is therefore a philosophy of the pure consciousness, a vision of essences (*Wesenheiten*).[2] But the vision of essences fails to reveal the mystery of existence. So does N. Hartmann's philosophy, with its idea of the 'trans-objective', and its most interesting ontological conception of the relation between the subject and the object.[3] Dilthey is much nearer to Existential philosophy when he refuses to resolve the spiritual life into its elements or to analyse it, and studies it, instead, as a whole in its synthetical aspects.[4]

[1] V. Solovyev, *La Critique des Principes abstraits* and *Les Principes philosophiques de la Connaissance intégrale.*

[2] Cf. Levinas, *La Théorie de l'Intuition dans la Phénoménologie de Husserl.*

[3] N. Hartmann, *Metaphysik der Erkenntnis.*

[4] Dilthey, *Einleitung in die Geisteswissenschaften,* etc. *Die geistige Welt. Einleitung in die Philosophie des Lebens.*

I shall now come to my personal conception of the subject in relation to the object. By opposing subject and object, intellection and Being, philosophical theory reaches an impasse, for it inevitably eliminates the subject from Being and makes Being objective. Thus, at a stroke, the subject becomes non-existential, and Being is identified with the object despite the fact that the object is the non-existential and ontic materialisation of the subject himself. In view of this, how can the problem of knowledge fail to be insolubly tragic? Man's apprehensive faculty is invariably confined to the outer fringe of Being. Is there no other solution except the primitive one of naïve realism? But this theory has very little to be said for it; it has no critical apparatus, it accepts the objective material world as the primary reality. For our purpose it would be a mistake to go back any further than Kant's *Critique of Pure Reason;* on the contrary, we should help the progression of philosophical theory by admitting that *knowledge is the apprehension of Being through Being*, that the knowing subject is not opposed to Being as to an object, but is an entity in himself. In other words, *the subject is existential*. The existential nature of the subject is one of the spiritual ways of apprehending the mystery of Being; it is an apprehension based not upon the outward opposition of philosophy and Being, but on their inward and intimate union. Thus true knowledge is an illumination of Being—an *Aufklärüng*, to restore the real sense of a term which the eighteenth century had degraded and falsified.

It is by affirming the existential nature of intellection that we attain to the concrete plane of existence as opposed to that of abstract Being. Hegel had already felt the necessity of effecting a passage from abstract Being—almost a synonym of non-Being—to concrete Being or to that existence which he envisaged as the union of Being and non-Being. He had already defined this state of union as the *Dasein*,[1] though he intended the term in a different sense from Heidegger. But he did, in fact, consider the problem of concrete knowledge and he did attempt to discard the traditional opposition of subject and object, while at the same time affirming the onto-logical nature of logic. The fundamental problem confronting philosophy is the nature of the relationship between the subject and the

[1] Hegel, *Enzyklopaedie der philosophischen Wissenschaften.* Torteil, *Wissenschaft der Logik. Die Lehre vom Sein.*

object when the subject is extraneous to objectively conceived Being. Attempts have been made to resolve this problem by affirming the identity of knowledge and Being, of subject and object. This identification restores the ontological dignity of knowledge, but fails to solve the problem. A more precise definition is necessary of the function of knowledge within Being. It must be shown that intellection is a creative act in the depths of Being, a flash of spontaneous light, a passage from darkness to light. But intellection is not simply the illumination of Being, it is the light itself in the innermost depths of Being. In fact, knowledge is immanent in Being, rather than Being in knowledge. But even if we do accept the identity of knowledge and Being, we shall have failed to consider the fundamental irrationality of Being, that is, we shall have imposed the idea of a rational Being.

In the depths of Being there is an obscure irrational substratum with which knowledge cannot be identified, but which it is its task to illuminate. Knowledge hovers on the brink of the dark abyss of Being, but it itself should remain lucid and clear. As we have already said, knowledge is immanent in Being; but what really takes place within Being is a *transcendence* and, in the process, a penetration into the vast depths beyond any given Being. The function of knowledge is not to reflect, but to create. Beyond any given stratum of Being there lies a still deeper stratum; and transcendence is the only means of attaining this deeper stratum of Being. The static notion of the *transcendental* should be replaced by the dynamic notion of *transcendence*. Simmel[1] very justifiably claims that the power to transcend is an essential property of life.

In Husserl, the *intentionality* of the subject can also be interpreted as a *transcendence* of the subject. But if this knowledge is understood as Being, as a function within and by means of Being, as a transcendence of Being operative in the heart of Being, then the knowing subject must necessarily be existential, and his knowledge must be immersed in the mystery of existence, in the depths of Being, rather than be a reflection of Objective Being. The participation of the knowing subject in existence is anterior to his knowledge. My existential experience is anterior to my knowledge. For that reason, knowledge is remembrance.

[1] Cf. Lebensanschauung.

Philosophy starts by doubting the reality of the perceptible world, of the world of objects and things; it inevitably sets out to criticize realism. But the critique of knowledge cannot always remain at the idealist stage. It must push its investigations further into the sphere of extra-objective existence, beyond the opposition of subject and object, beyond the perceptible world. This sphere of primary life is that of the existing and of existence—but not that of the thing itself, which is but a product knowledge, the limit-concept of thought; nor that of objective realities. We are using the term *existence* here in preference to that of *life*, because *life* is a biological category, as we can see in Nietzsche and Bergson, whereas *existence* is an onto-logical category. To exist, is for man to dwell within himself, in his own authentic world, rather than to be at the mercy of the social and biological world. As opposed to any philosophy of life, that of Klages, for example, Existential philosophy is ontological rather than biological; and it is related to spiritual philosophy at both its extremes. It is the philosophy of destiny, of its intimacy and its re-lationship with concrete universality. It is never satisfied merely to consider the general and the objective processes of the external world, for philosophical theory should above all be concerned with the thinking subject and his existence. But objective thought appears to take no interest in him, and that is why it often unwittingly objectifies the subjective and, therefore, human existence. We are thus confronted with the fundamental problem: What is objectifi-cation? How can we attain the existing or existence in an objective world? Man's future destiny, the possibility even of philosophy, depends on the solution of this problem.

It is important to grasp, first of all, that the objective world is a degraded and spellbound world—a world of phenomena rather than one of existences. Objective processes *abstract* and disrupt existence. They substitute society for community, general principles for com-munion, and the empire of Caesar for the Kingdom of God. There is no participation in objective processes; for, as we shall see more precisely hereafter, the result of objectification in knowledge as else-where is not only to isolate man but also to confine his activities to an essentially alien world. Objective processes are a spiritual mani-festation, but there is no spiritual freedom in the resulting objective world. Reality is originally part of the inner existence, of the inner

[44]

spiritual communion and community, but it becomes degraded in the process of objectification and of having to submit to social necessities. Thus, although we are considering objectification only in its relation to knowledge, we can affirm that there is no spiritual mystery in the objective world.

Can it be maintained that objective knowledge is in itself deficient and sinful? Can we regard it, as Shestov does, as the cause of degradation in the world? That would be to propagate a serious error. *The state of sin, of deficiency and of degradation, should be attributed to Being rather than to knowledge.* In its degraded state knowledge can only apprehend an already degraded Being. But objective knowledge still reveals something of true reality despite its divorce from the intimate existence and the spiritual world. Objective processes suppose a degraded world, an abstraction and a determinism, but it is nevertheless possible to have some knowledge of the degraded world.

There are degrees of objective knowledge. Natural science has the greatest degree of objectivity; it is detached from man's intimate existence and is a form of knowledge most appropriate to the physico-mathematical sciences. Its degree of objectivity is such that the object of knowledge appears to be completely divorced from the subject's inner existence. Mathematics are no doubt a manifestation of the creative spirit and, like all other branches of knowledge, they imply a spiritual process such as that postulated in Brunschvicg's central idea. This is a very valuable form of knowledge in which the *Logos* is reflected. Nevertheless, the objective processes at work therein hamper the spirit and make the inner mystery of existence inaccessible. In this sense science is not ontological, as Meyerson maintained it to be. At another degree, the knowledge of the social world is also objective. It has the advantage of illuminating the entire objective process, which is essentially a social one; for, as we shall see, *objective knowledge derives from the social sphere, whereas existential knowledge derives from the sphere of communion.*

Any degree of objective knowledge is invariably abstracted from the existential or human subject. It is indisputable that the existential subject is a part of Being—of non-objective Being, because the subject himself determines objective processes by virtue of his life in the degraded world. The existential subject should never be identified

[45]

with the biological, the sociological or the psychological subject, because they are merely the products of objective reasoning. Naturalism is such a product. It contains a degree of objective truth but its claim to universal validity is false because it represents only the material aspect of a whole variety of Being. There are naturalist tendencies even in theology, and they play a too important part by interpreting God objectively and by claiming knowledge of Him by analogy with objects and natural phenomena. The fact, however, that human existence can be in communion with the Divine existence is evidence that God is not a natural object or a part of the objective world. If it were otherwise, I could not be a part of Him. True philosophical knowledge always contains objective elements; but its real aim is to transcend objectivity so as to be able then to investigate the purpose of Being. *It is the prerogative of the spirit to discover the purpose of matter itself.*

We must admit then that naturalist metaphysics, since it is concerned primarily with substances, is only a type of objective philosophical knowledge. In its attempt to be extra-human, it objectifies God, the spirit, the soul and the understanding. To-day, philosophical naturalism is on the decline because it fails to attribute any significance to human existence in the natural and objective worlds. The great philosophers have always admitted this fact, even when they have expressed themselves in terms of naturalist metaphysics. Socrates, Saint Augustine, Descartes and Spinoza were concerned above all with the intimate Ego. Kant almost achieved Existential philosophy as a result of the distinction he established between the sphere of nature and that of freedom. By means of this distinction between the inner and the outer spheres of existence he helped largely to discredit both naïve realism and objective rationalism. But he failed to be the founder of the new Existential philosophy because his phenomenalism was unsound.

In his attempt to arrive at freedom, Plotinus had already endeavoured to transcend the objective world.[1] To pass beyond objective naturalism is equivalent, in philosophy, to passing beyond conceptualist metaphysics;[2] for a concept is formulated about an

[1] Cf. Brehier, *La Philosophie de Plotin.*

[2] Windelband and Rickert are well aware of this; but they make the mistake of thinking that normativism is a solution for philosophy.

[46]

object, and an objective process consists precisely in a conceptual elaboration. This transcendence controverts the erroneous notion that thought can be distinct from sentiment. Far from apprehending Being, objective knowledge is nothing more than a rationalization of irrational Being. As Jaspers has grasped so well, the mystery of existence can only be interpreted by means of metaphors and symbols. No concept is able to reveal the purpose of existence or its underlying values. The existential mystery revealing purpose is that wherein the subject and the predicate are identified. I *am*; but another's Ego *is*, God *is*, the divine world *is*. The existential sphere is also the personal sphere. There is nothing general, nothing abstract in it. Just as God is manifest in the subject rather than in the object, so the personality is revealed in the existential subject. Both the divine and the human elements are absent from the objective world; and to objectify God is to make Him neither divine nor human. The sphere of civilization is still the sphere of existence, although the existential and creative subject is kept in the background. Thus civilization is not the ultimate reality, for it is dedicated to death and the last judgment. Even the artistic perception of the object involves an objective process, because it fails to realize that union in which the object is transcended.

Culture represents a different degree of objectification than either nature or society. But it is very largely dominated by essentially objective social forms. In the process of building up culture man's creative activity is degraded and subjected to law.[1] Any degree of objectification implies the rule of law as opposed to that of Grace. That is its religious justification. But religion and theology are objective processes in so far as they are social manifestations. The purpose of religious life is to enable men to pass beyond the limits of the objective world, beyond the rule of law, beyond social and natural necessity; but historical religion cannot escape its social and objective ties. And as a result, religion gives rise to society instead of communion; it becomes a slave of the State and can therefore be interpreted from the sociological point of view. For that reason, religion is not the ultimate revelation or expression of man's communion with the divine world.[2] The prophetic principle in religion

[1] Cf. my book, *The Meaning of Creation*.
[2] Karl Barth has made some very just observations about this.

implies a breaking away from the objective world. The Church is social and objective, on the one hand, and communion and authentic existence, on the other. And that is the whole difficulty of the problem. It disrupts all human life and knowledge. Knowledge is objectification; it is also the consciousness of objective processes and it is, therefore, a means of transcending the objective world and of attaining the spiritual world. Dualism is the fundamental truth underlying philosophy, but it is not the ultimate ontological truth.

Knowledge is often identified with rationalization. It is true that the latter plays an important part in knowledge; but rationalization not only implies objectification and abstraction, but also the development of general principles at the expense of communion and participation. As we have often noted, rational knowledge is unable to grasp the individual and singular aspects of Being. If, as we have seen, objectification is a synonym of division, this fact is confirmed in the general concept.

Knowledge poses the problem of the irrational with which it is inevitably confronted. German philosophy was the first to investigate this problem seriously, to attempt a rational interpretation of the irrational. The light of reason had to illuminate the mystery of the irrational; but that need not imply that reason should be strictly rational, for reason is not limited to the *ratio*, but also comprehends the *Logos*. To admit the limitations of reason when confronted with irrational Being, to admit its paradoxical and contradictory nature, is not merely to discover the weakness but also the strength of reason and knowledge. But mere rationalization is a weakness in so far as it demonstrates that reason is unable to transcend its limitations. But since the whole strength of reason lies in its power to transcend itself, its highest achievement is *docta ignorantia,* apophatic knowledge.[1] There is an immanent as well as a transcendental aspect in knowledge; but the act of transcending is immanent in knowledge, it is an act of knowledge.

To objectify is to rationalize in the sense of accepting concepts— substances, universal ideas and the rest—as realities. Rational and objective thought is abstracted from the spheres of the irrational and of the individual, of existence and of the existing. We should distinguish above all between two types of knowledge: there is, first

[1] Nicolas of Cusa, *Von der Wissenschaft des Nichtwissen.*

of all, rational and objective knowledge which is confined within the frontiers of reason and apprehends only the general; and secondly, there is the knowledge immanent in Being and in existence through which reason is enabled to apprehend the irrational and the individual after transcending the general; this knowledge is synonymous with *community* and participation. Both these types of knowledge are to be found in the history of human thought. Knowledge can thus be considered from two different standpoints: from that of society, of communication between men by means of the objective and the general; and from that of community, of existential communion and of penetration into the heart of the individual.

This is the very core of my thought. Objective knowledge is invariably *social*, because it fails to apprehend the existential subject; its essential nature, which is to be universally valid, is social and depends on its degree of community. A sociology of knowledge has still to be elaborated;[1] but it will have to be interpreted in a different way from positivism, since it is a metaphysical discipline for which the problem of society, of communion, and of community, is the ultimate problem of Being. Being can be communion and participation; or it can be society and communication. The idea that all the spheres of Being should be rationalized and socialized is an erroneous and completely anti-Christian one. It is the result of scientism rather than science, of the attempt to universalize degrees and forms of knowledge of which the validity is strictly limited.

A knowledge founded on scientific principles and on organized social forms is unable to achieve unity or monism; any unity thus arrived at would be extra-existential, definitely objectified and abstracted. The ultimate unity in which all contradictions and antinomies are resolved, is attainable only by means of apophatic knowledge—that absolute knowledge which brings about communion with God and the Kingdom of God. In the degraded world, all speculation about God is cataphic; in objective society there is always dualism, the confrontation of two principles, contradiction, tragedy. The whole problem is to discover whether the ultimate unity, harmony and community, can only be realized on the higher apophatic

[1] Cf. Max Scheller, *Die Wissenschaft und die Gesellschaft. Probleme einer Soziologie des Wissens*. This book is valuable as an exposition of the problem, but it is not entirely satisfactory. Simmel's work is also important in this connection.

plane; or whether they can also be realized on the lower cataphic plane, as rationalism, positivism, scientism and communism, all agree to maintain.

The problem of knowledge and that of society are here very closely interrelated. In this respect the Marxian analysis was right. Until recently philosophy has not paid sufficient attention to the correspondence between the degree of knowledge and that of community. If it considered the problem at all, it was in the form of sociological positivism and historical materialism which attributed to sociology the validity of a universal science.

But let us consider the sociology of knowledge on a higher and metaphysic plane. The development of knowledge helps to make for a greater community, since knowledge is related to man's degree of consciousness, which is itself related to the degree of community. But authentic community is only to be found in the heart of authentic existence, at the point where it becomes one not only with objective society, but also with communion. Communion is a spiritual rather than a natural phenomenon. By virtue of it knowledge is transformed; for man's attitude to his fellow-beings will change if he becomes conscious of his intimate existence, and of his fellow-beings as an Ego or a Thou instead of as an object. And as knowledge will learn to regard man in this light, so the community will be transfigured.

Philosophy is concerned primarily with man's inner life, and it should therefore investigate all problems from the standpoint of human knowledge. The purpose of existence cannot be elucidated either from things or from objects; it is inherent in the knowing subject and in existence itself. Thus purely rational philosophy, as an objective process, cannot apprehend the purpose of existence which is immanent in the depths of Being. Unfortunately, degraded Being is at the mercy of objective processes abstracting it from authentic existence, so that it interprets existence in purely material forms such as hunger, economic necessity (as in Marx), the libido, sexual desire (as in Freud), anxiety and fear (as in Heidegger).

It also follows that, since knowledge is essentially immaterial, its ability to apprehend the material nature of things and objects remains the great enigma. In the philosophy of Saint Thomas Aquinas this problem is one of intellection. It can only be resolved if we admit the *ontic* nature of knowledge, that it participates in Being, illuminating its obscure depths and integrating the objective world in the spiritual. The faith in the immutability of natural laws, which goes back to Greek geometry, is only a faith in reason as a manifestation of nature's inherent spirituality. This spirituality is oppressed by the objective world; but we apprehend it as our destiny as soon as we become converted to the inner world of existence. Thus, the so-called natural laws are actually human destiny.

When we use the term *existential subject*, we are merely adopting the terminology of a current philosophy of knowledge. But this terminology is not the definitive one. Existence is not fully realized until we can pass from the subject to the human personality. Existential philosophy is a Personalist philosophy; the human personality is the real subject of knowledge. We must therefore consider the question: Is knowledge a creative act of the human personality and does it suppose the personality's freedom?

KNOWLEDGE AND FREEDOM—INTELLECTUAL ACTIVITY AND THE CREATIVE ESSENCE OF KNOWLEDGE—ACTIVE AND PASSIVE KNOWLEDGE—THEORETICAL AND PRACTICAL KNOWLEDGE

It is impossible to maintain that the intellectual subject is absolutely passive or that he merely reflects the object. The object does not penetrate the subject as one might enter a room. A realism of this kind lacks consistency; it cannot explain, for example, how such a material thing as an object can be transformed into knowledge, into an intellectual and spiritual event, in the subject, if the intellectual subject were entirely passive and knowledge but the reflection and peculiar activity of the object. The fact that the subject, in the process of intellection, is capable of transforming the object into knowledge is sufficient proof of his inherent activity. The process of intellection discovers the meaning, the cosmos, underlying the meaningless and chaotic universe. It does not create another superfluous reality, but rather adds to the existing reality, which thereby assumes a greater significance. It is essentially creative and promotes organization by helping the human mind to master chaos and the obscurities of existence; in a word, to master the world both theoretically and practically by the exercise of the human faculties of creation and application.

The activity of the knowing subject manifests itself in two ways: firstly, by objectification—a process which helps the subject to orientate himself in a dark and degraded world, wherein the mystery of existence is obscured and wherein the subject is forced to make his submission to the world. Technology is the supreme result of knowledge thus objectified. At the same time, the fact of objectification contradicts the idea that the subject is passively penetrated by the object. Therefore the objectified world cannot be, as is often affirmed, a purely objective world. It is a real world, one possessed of a certain degree of reality, of a certain state of Being; but, above all, it is a world which manifests the activity of the creative subject and the reciprocal action of the knowing subject and the object known. Secondly, the subject can orientate himself by means of Existential philosophy, which dispenses with objectification: the human subject does not apprehend the object, but the revelation of human existence and, through it, that of the divine world. Thus in the light of Existential philosophy, knowledge is both active and creative, though in a somewhat different way. It can illuminate the objective world wherein *meaning* is revealed, the meaning of human existence and of the universe as part of the Divine Being. But all revelation of meaning is the result of spiritual activity, of the integral rather than the partial reason. To apprehend existence is to illuminate it and to make it significant, to illuminate Being, and consequently to regenerate and to enrich it with hitherto undiscerned elements.

The creative nature of intellectual activity differs in the natural and the spiritual sciences.[1] In the former, creative activity is governed by mathematical laws and is confined to the processes of objectification; in the latter, it is concerned with probing the meaning of existence. William James was right when he stated that knowledge was not the result of an act, but was itself an act. Indeed, it could not be otherwise, since knowledge is a spiritual emanation. Knowledge is as dynamic in its non-social contemplative form as when it actively transfigures the world. These are only two of the ways in which it exercises its creative power; for just as spiritual activity draws strength from contemplation, from an eternal source, so contemplation in its turn supposes a spiritual origin. Thus in Plotinus, the soul, as the superior, organizes the inferior world; in the same way, contemplation is not merely a passive reflection of Being. We cannot seriously believe that only the object of knowledge and of contemplation is endowed with energy, since God Himself ceases to be a free agent when objectified. Activity is the exclusive property of the subject; and God is an agent only when He is a subject, a spiritual essence revealed by the subject. The connection between knowledge and magic is not far-fetched, for it ultimately gave rise to science. The pursuit of knowledge has always been a virile, forceful and conquering occupation. Technology is the magic of to-day,

[1] Cf. the work by Dilthey we have already quoted.

just as primitive magic was the technology of the primitive peoples. But the exercise of magic involves objectification, the abstraction of the subject and his identification with the object; it is essentially naturalistic and aims at satisfying the human urge to dominate the environment. This distinguishes it from the essentially spiritualistic nature of mysticism, on the one hand, and from religion which, despite its objective elements, inspires piety and veneration rather than awe, on the other hand.

But we cannot meditate ont he creative nature of human knowledge without having to consider further the question of intuition and creation. Thus we must ask ourselves whether intuition, considered as the highest form of knowledge, is a creative act, or whether it is merely a passive reflection of reality? As defined in the contemporary philosophies of Husserl, Bergson and Lossky,[1] intuition is passive. Husserl affirms that intuition is the vision of essences (*Wesenheiten*) which the knowing subject in his extra-human abstraction suffers to invade him. Bergson maintains that intellection is an active building up of the spatial universe (*objectification* in my terminology), whereas the intuitive penetration of duration is passive. And finally, Lossky critically reconstitutes naïve realism by making his realities participate directly in intellection. I maintain, on the contrary, that intuition is essentially active. It is the essence of creative activity in the depths of knowledge, and it postulates creative inspiration. Intuition is admittedly active in the sphere of natural science: it should therefore be all the more active in the sphere of spiritual science. Intuition gives birth to meaning; it is the irruption of meaning in the dark regions of Being, a flash of lightning forking the night. Greek philosophy must be held responsible for confronting the intellect passively with the objective world of Ideas; this fact, of course, prevented Greek philosophy from evolving the notion of intuition, and restricted the researches of Scholastic philosophy which carried on the Hellenic tradition.

Bergson, while maintaining that intuition is passive, nevertheless establishes a clear distinction between knowledge as a part of active and creative duration, and knowledge as a part of those solidified realities within which duration is congealed.[2] The creative agency of

---

[1] Cf. N. Lossky, *De L'intuitivisme.*
[2] Cf. Jankelevitch's fine book, *Bergson.*

[54]

the knowing subject participating in Being and existence, the dynamic life of this Being and of this existence, all constitute a change in and not merely a new way of interpreting Being. As everybody will agree, the best evidence of the creative power of knowledge is afforded by the new valuation it places on Being. We may ask, what is the origin of this activity? And also, what enables knowledge to illuminate and to put a higher valuation on Being? Knowledge would remain unintelligible unless the existential subject were endowed with a certain measure of freedom.

There are two aspects of knowledge. The first is its creative aspect, manifest in the free agency of the existential subject, who is not in any way determined by the known Being, who is anterior to Being, and who is absolutely original. In the process of intellection this subjective freedom allies itself with the *Logos*. But the *Logos* is divinely inspired, whereas subjective freedom originates in the irrational abyss prior to any Being. Thus knowledge is not merely the reflection of Being in the subject in the form of speculative knowledge, but also necessarily the creative reaction of the subject's illumined freedom to Being, as a result of which Being is modified. The freedom implicit in the exercise of knowledge receives its illumination from the *Logos*. But it is also related to the Eros. To pursue knowledge without any consciousness of love, merely to seek power, is a form of demonism. It may therefore be affirmed that knowledge is essentially cosmogonic. It should consider reality carefully and examine it conscientiously; for moral pathos is the true inspiration and urge of our quest of truth. The subjective freedom thus generated by the *Logos* transfigures reality. The nature of knowledge is conjugal; it is both male and female, it is the conjunction of these two principles, the impregnation of the feminine element by virile meaning.

The basis of knowledge is irrational because it is derived from a pre-ontic freedom. The irrational foundation of rational knowledge has been most clearly grasped by the German metaphysicians of the school of Boehme. Another creative aspect is the humanization of Being implied in man's cognitive activity. The humanization is particularly manifest in *cataphic* knowledge, where it may sometimes result in evil. In *apophatic* knowledge, on the other hand, there is a limit to this humanizing process, a limit beyond which created Being is transcended and made divine. To admit the free agency of the existential subject in the intellectual sphere is to uphold a philosophy affirming the primacy of freedom over Being. Thus voluntarism is given precedence over intellectualism, though we must bear in mind the fact that the will is never absolutely a free agent. Intellectualist philosophy, whether Platonic or Aristotelian, invariably involves the negation of intellectual freedom and thus neutralizes its essentially creative nature. Every intellectualist system is founded upon an external principle, upon a determination, which allows the rational and objective Being to determine entirely the process of intellection and the mode of subjective apprehension. Intellectualist philosophy is thus inevitably forced to deny the validity of the subject and its participation in the mystery of existence. *Freedom is the essential condition of the existential subject.* As it is, the underlying tragedy of philosophy, which is engendered by the primacy of freedom over Being, of the existential subject over the object, escapes intellectualist philosophy. A purely intellectualist system is unable to recognize error or falsehood, since it apprehends truth by virtue of necessity. Thus Descartes, in order to explain the possibility of error, had to resort to the notion of the will and of the free agent, although his philosophy was still largely based upon the intellectualist conception. The inherent freedom of intellection not only makes it a creative process, but also the source of many errors, blunders and insurmountable contradictions, which only the Divine Grace can reconcile.

When we affirm the creative nature of intellection, we must be careful not to make the relationship between the Creator and the creature depend upon causality, that is, upon necessity rather than upon freedom. In reality, however, there are degrees of freedom and necessity corresponding to the various types of knowledge, to the situation of the existential subject in the hierarchy of Being. The structure of the human consciousness is not immutable.[1] Thus objective and naturalist types of philosophy are far more prone to accept the law of necessity than metaphysics, which is chiefly orientated towards non-objectified and spiritual forms of existence. Intellectual freedom manifested itself first of all in natural science, which was mostly preoccupied with the degraded world. The scientific con-

[1] Cf. Berdyaev, *Freedom and the Spirit* (Geoffrey Bles).

ception of the world demonstrates the practical application of knowledge to the natural world in the form of technical supremacy over nature; but actually this conception is engendered by the free spiritual agency of the scientist or inventor. It is the spirit which organizes matter; but the scientist, by concentrating merely on material rather than on spiritual things, tends to be progressively involved in the degradation of his original freedom. Creative inspiration is the highest form of freedom; labour is the lowest and most material form.

This fact makes the philosophy of labour particularly important not only from the social and moral, but also from the intellectual standpoint. Sociology[1] is responsible for investigating the theoretical aspects of labour. *Homo sapiens* is also *homo faber*; the knowing subject cannot apprehend without acting or working. Both the origin and aim of knowledge are creative; but creation involves labour, and is accordingly related, as Marx had observed, to social forms of labour. But Marx failed to understand the essentially spiritual nature of labour, and he degraded this truth by his purely materialistic interpretation. Labour is a spiritual phenomenon; the connection between knowledge and labour or vital activity is determined by the existential nature of the subject. This fact demonstrates the abnormal tendencies of both science and philosophy when they confine themselves exclusively to academic and abstract considerations. The only effect of such misapplication is to pervert knowledge. When philosophy abstracts itself from life, from existence as a whole, as is the case of the Russian thinker N. Feodorov, it tends to establish a false set of values. The knowing subject, on the other hand, must by virtue of his existential quality necessarily reconcile intellect and will, contemplation and labour, theory and practice. Thus Existential philosophy is by its nature both theoretical and practical. Its aim is to study the unifying principle which integrates philosophy and the community of men, and also to demonstrate the social character of logical communication. For this reason, my principal endeavour in this book has been to establish the relationship between knowledge as an instrument of objectified society and knowledge as a means of achieving existential communion.

[1] Max Scheller and Simmel in his *Sociologie* have many valuable comments to offer on this relationship.

CHAPTER IV

THE DEGREES OF INTELLECTUAL COMMUNITY—THE EXTINCTION OF THE WORLD OF THINGS AND OBJECTS AND THE APPROACH TO THE ENIGMA OF EXISTENCE

Philosophical theory has not yet thrown sufficient light on the social content of knowledge, on the intellectual ties which unite men and make their mutual comprehension possible. Through knowledge man is enabled to escape from his self-confinement. It also helps him to overcome the disintegration resulting from the spatial and temporal division of the world, to transport himself into the remote past or another sphere of existence; it is, in fact, a unifying force in a disintegrated world. The social aspect of knowledge is universally valid, *allgemeingultig*; and logic itself, as the basis of intellectual communication, is likewise social in character. The very necessity of subjecting thought to the laws of logic is a social necessity; for thought is originally founded upon intuition, which is a personal and anthropocentric revelation of the mystery of Being. But the material results of knowledge are social, intended for communication, since the very fact of publishing a scientific discovery or of writing a book is a social phenomenon.

The degree of communication attainable by knowledge is largely dependent on the degree of community existing among men. Since intellectual objectification involves socialization, it must vary with the different social groups. By reason of their peculiar structures, the various social groups refract the objective and universal data of knowledge in their own way. Scientific knowledge has, until the present day, been the contribution of specialists, of University men, but its discoveries, especially those of the physico-mathematical sciences, have been used as a means of communication between men of very different spiritual outlooks. Thus scientific knowledge, of which the mathematical and physical sciences represent the pure type, provides a universal means of communication between men, but without at the same time establishing any true communion between them. In reality, although the truths propounded by the mathematical and physical sciences constitute a basis of agreement between men of the most varied spiritual outlooks, religious beliefs, social classes, nationality and culture, they imply the lowest level of true human communion. Its universal and abstract quality makes science the appropriate mode of communication in the spiritually disintegrated, objective and social world. A certain degree of community between men, such as that, for example, expressed in the symbolism of a language,[1] is an essential basis for communication and for the propagation of intellectual discoveries; but this degree of community may co-exist with spiritual disunion. This is the problem confronting sociology. The social aspects of knowledge, though divorced from the inner existence and from communion, are those which command the greatest attention and which are the most widely diffused. On the other hand, communal knowledge, which participates in the mystery of Being and in the spiritual life, is not universally accepted or used as a current means of communication.

Philosophical truths suppose a far greater degree of spiritual community than physico-mathematical truths; but the greatest degree of spiritual community is to be found in religious truths. These truths appear to be absolutely *subjective*, undemonstrable, without proof, incapable of providing the foundation of a universal community. But they acquire within the spiritual community or the Church a far greater universality than the mathematical truths, because they suppose faith and unanimity on the part of the faithful. Thus in the Middle Ages, when Christianity reached its greatest degree of objectification, Christian mankind constituted a community for which Christian truths possessed a universal validity, whereas scientific truths had not yet acquired their social currency and inspired scandalized apprehension rather than conviction. In our day it is the discoveries of science which are the most socially objectified, and the scientific modes of communication which are the most generalized, whereas religious truths appear to be *subjective*.

The means of human communication are related to the degree of human community. The conditions of our degraded and disinte-

[1] Cf. Delacroix, *Le Langage et la Pensée*.

grated world tend to make the maximum social objectification the basis of universal communication. But the degraded and disintegrated state of the world cannot be directly the result of the material application of scientific discoveries, but is inherent in the very constitution of Being. In our divided world, science has acquired the validity and universality of law. This universal validity is not shared by philosophy as we have defined it, by Existential philosophy, since it is not concerned with the objective world. Objectivity is necessarily confined to the object. On the other hand, subjectivity is neither false nor contrary to the truth, but can attain the maximum of truth; it lacks, however, that character of universal validity which is the essential condition of communication.

Spiritual community or communion would therefore appear to be an inadequate basis of communication between men. That is, indeed, one of the paradoxical aspects of knowledge as manifest in the degraded world. These means of communication based upon spatial and temporal disintegration are derived from objectified knowledge without regard for true communion, from mathematical truths rather than from the immediate apprehension of Being and existence. Thus, what we call *religion* or *bond* has served not only as a means to communion, but also as an instrument of social organization and mystification. This perversion of religion is the result of the objectifying processes at work upon revealed truths. The means of communication thus elaborated by religion[1] have no foundation of true community. Only the spiritual life can obviate the social implications of objectification, but its revealed truths are in no wise universally valid. The degree of objectification varies with the physical, organic and social worlds.[2] Thus, we must note that, although objectification is primarily a socializing process, sociological data are not so universally accepted as scientific data. This can be explained by the fact that sociology is dependent upon man's social and communal position, and above all upon his peculiar psychology. The physico-mathematical sciences have therefore a much greater universal and

[1] Cf. Berdyaev, *The Destiny of Man* (Geoffrey Bles) and Bergson, *The Two Sources of Morality and Religion.*

[2] An existential apprehension of the social world is possible. Thus Marx's interpretation of capitalism from the standpoint *of its social relations is existential. His materialism, on the other hand, is an extreme form of objectification.*

social validity. Marxist theory, for example, finds it more difficult to attribute 'class' associations to these sciences than to sociological doctrines.

It should be the aim of any concrete philosophy to integrate the social aspects of knowledge and to lay the foundations of a sociological philosophy. A philosophy of this kind would help to throw light on religious philosophy; a sociological philosophy could be made to comprehend a gnosiology of the Church, since the Church can also be a sociological category. Nevertheless, a theory of socially objectified knowledge, comprehending every degree of community from the particular to the universal, can be truly illuminated only by Existential philosophy, when envisaged in the light of the existential subject. Thus the objective world, the solid and inert world of matter, wherein the idea of universality is but a social phenomenon, will dissolve into nothing when confronted with the revelation of the mystery of existence, with the spiritual, extra-natural revelation animating both the depths and the heights of Being. We shall have to investigate the same problem when dealing with the Ego's solitude in relation to society.

THIRD MEDITATION

THE EGO, SOLITUDE AND SOCIETY

CHAPTER I

THE EGO AND SOLITUDE—SOLITUDE
AND SOCIABILITY

The Ego is primitive; it can be neither deduced from nor reduced to anything. When I say 'I', no philosophical doctrine is expressed or postulated. Nor does the Ego constitute the substance of either religion or metaphysics. The error of Descartes' affirmation, *cogito ergo sum,* consists in his attempt to deduce the Ego's existence from something—and in the fact that he did finally deduce it from thought. In reality, however, I am not because I think, but I think because I am. It is not true to say, 'I think, therefore I am'; but rather, 'I am surrounded on all sides by impenetrable infinity, and therefore I think'. I am, in the first place. The Ego belongs to the sphere of existence.

The Ego is primarily existential, and only secondarily an object; it is synonymous with freedom. As Amiel has very rightly pointed out, the essential nature of the Ego can never become objective.[1] It cannot become an object precisely because it is the Ego. As soon as it does become an object it ceases to be an Ego. It is an existential and not a natural phenomenon. It is primary and primitive.[2] Consciousness is merely inherent in it, like unconsciousness. The primitive Ego is rooted in existence, and not in consciousness as many philosophers would have us suppose. Consciousness already implies a degree of objectivity. Maine de Biran makes a very important contribution when he argues that conscious endeavour is the dawn of the personality; but that is not the Ego's primary characteristic. It has also been affirmed that self-consciousness is synonymous with self-creation.[3] There is a great deal of truth in this affirmation; but it postulates the existence of something anterior to consciousness.

The birth of consciousness is a very important event in the Ego's destiny. The unity of this consciousness is liable to be quickly dis-

[1] Amiel, *Fragments d'un Journal intime.*   [2] Cf. J. Chevalier, *Bergson.*
[3] Louis Lavelle, *La Conscience de soi.*

rupted and the Ego to be isolated, but it constantly endeavours to re-integrate itself and to overcome its isolation. The Ego's development is along the path of freedom; but extreme self-consciousness is inseparable from a feeling of bondage and dependence upon the non-Ego. Originally there was no line of demarcation between the Ego and the 'totality'; later, when the existence of the non-Ego was revealed, the Ego developed in contact with it a particularly acute and anguished sensibility. The distinction often established between the 'I' and the Ego, the *anima* and the *animus*, is a secondary one connected with the Ego's spiritual growth.[1] The stages of its development are as follows: firstly, the undifferentiated unity of the Ego with the universe; secondly, the dualist opposition of the Ego and the non-Ego; thirdly and finally, the achievement of the concrete union of every Ego with the Thou, a union which preserves plurality in a transfigured form.

The Ego is the source and origin of philosophy, which springs from doubt as to the nature of the objective world. The philosopher's consciousness is not of a collective, *generic* type; nor can he admit as his premise an Ego that is objectively identified with the collective consciousness. Formerly, men used to live in a comparatively confined space, which prevented them from experiencing a sense of solitude. To-day, they are on the whole beginning to live in the great universe, in the midst of immensity, in the perspective of a boundless horizon, which only inspires them with a growing sense of isolation and abandonment. But the universe and its infinite horizon have always been the philosopher's domain; his vision has always transcended the frontiers of the immediate world; and for that reason he has, like the prophet, been always solitary. The philosopher has no need to identify himself with the collective consciousness in order to overcome this solitude; he can achieve this by the pursuit of knowledge. We shall investigate this aspect of the problem in greater detail later on.

An immutable essence in the process of mutation is an antinomian definition of the Ego. For unless there existed a subject of mutation, a subject capable of preserving his identity in the process of change, the Ego could not suffer a temporal change or actualize itself. But the Ego does preserve its identity and uniqueness despite its ever

[1] Cf. Henri Brémond, *Prière et Poésie.*

[66]

changing aspect. It may contract or expand; there is a smaller and greater Ego inherent in all of us. The Ego may, therefore, be defined as the constant unity underlying all change, as the extra-temporal centre that can only be defined in terms of itself. But while the Ego's variations can be determined objectively, its essence cannot be thus determined. It is self-determining; it determines itself from within when responding actively to all external influences.

All Egos resemble each other in that each is unique and distinct. Each Ego is an entity, a world in itself, postulating the existence of other Egos without seeking to identify itself with them. The Ego I have in mind is the extra-social and non-objective Ego. The Ego's existence precedes its materialization in this world; and yet it is inseparable from the existence of the Other Self and of other Egos.

Self-consciousness implies consciousness of others; it is social in the depths of its metaphysical nature. Man's life, in so far as it is the expression of the Ego's, presupposes the existence of other men, of the world, and of God. The Ego's absolute isolation, its refusal to communicate with anything outside it, with the Thou, would be suicidal. The Ego's existence is threatened whenever it denies the potential existence within itself of another Ego, or of the Thou. As Amiel has very justly said, the Ego's phenomenological process is the means by which the mystery of the universe is revealed to it. Fichte's Ego is not authentic, because it is universal rather than individual, and because it postulates the non-Ego rather than another Ego or the Thou. The Ego becomes conscious of itself as the product of its own activity; but this activity is based upon the existence of something and of someone else as well as upon that of the active Ego. But we are primarily concerned here with the existence of another Ego, of the Thou.

The Ego is compounded of both body and soul. The dualistic theory of body and soul is a perfectly sterile one. The body participates in both the inner and objective spheres of existence. The inner world does not depend upon its exterior manifestation, it is *per se* a revelation of another state of Being. The problem of the Ego, and of its relationship to other Egos or to the object, has its origin precisely in this sphere of Being, which is distinct from that we term the 'life-in-this-world'. It may be a matter of surprise that consciousness, and especially self-consciousness, is associated with a

[67]

state of suffering, vulnerability and disruption. This state of suffering
is related to what certain philosophers, like Simmel, Tillich, Jaspers,
have termed man's 'limit-situation'. It is true that the Ego is exteri-
orized and that it obeys the laws of the objective world; but its
allegiance to this world is only partial. Human life is in the process
of constantly transcending itself; but the fact of man's materialization, however partial, in the objective world makes his existence a
torture and a torment to him. The Ego's reality lies in its endeavour
to transcend itself. It perishes as soon as it can find no further outlet
for itself. That constitutes the Ego's fundamental enigma.

To realize itself, the Ego must fulfil two conditions: firstly, it must
never be merely an objective or social instrument; and secondly, it
must always endeavour to transcend itself. In the process of transcending itself it tends to emerge from its seclusion and to unite with
the Other Self, with other Egos, with the Thou, with its fellow-
men, with the divine world. There is nothing so detestable or destructive as egocentricity, as an Ego absorbed in itself, and in its own
states, oblivious of other Egos, of the world, of its plurality and
'totality'; in a word, an Ego that fails to transcend itself. Such a state
resembles the condition of certain hysterical women. Only a lyrical
poet is capable of creating something beautiful out of such an un-
natural state, and in this sense poetical creation is a manner of
transcending.

The problem of solitude, which has so far been given very little
philosophical consideration, throws a great deal of light on the Ego.
It has also a distinct bearing on the problem of knowledge, which,
of course, helps to transcend solitude and to achieve inner illumination. The Ego's failure to establish a relationship with the We, and
the acute and anguished sense of solitude resulting therefrom, gives
birth to the personality's growing consciousness of itself.[1] The mass
of mankind is quite untroubled by this sense of solitude, which is
stifled by the primitive collective and its generic mode of life. The
sense of solitude springs from man's endeavour to develop his personality regardless of the life of the species. Only when man is alone,
when he is overwhelmed by a distressing sense of his isolation, does
he become aware of his personality, of his originality, of his singu-

[1] For solitude and communion, consult Lavelle's interesting chapter in his book,
La Conscience de soi.

larity and uniqueness, of his distinctness from everyone and everything else. An extreme sense of solitude tends to make everything else appear alien and heterogeneous. Man feels himself to be a stranger, an alien without a spiritual home. This feeling of spiritual exile is excellently expressed in the Orphic conception of the origin of the soul:

> And long in the world did she pine,
> Consumed with most wondrous desires;
> Nor could plaintive earth's sad songs dim
> Her remembrance of heavenly lyres.
>
> LERMONTOV

As long as man does not feel himself at home in the world of his authentic existence, as long as he sees other men in the light of this alien world, he can only conceive the world, and the men in it, as objects reflecting the objectified world of necessity. But the objective world can never be the means of liberating man from the prison of his solitude. Thus the fundamental truth holds good: no objective relationship can help the Ego along the path of freedom and communion, whatever their relationship. In the depths of his solitude, of his hermetic existence, man grows acutely aware of his personality, originality and singularity. He also longs to escape from his solitary confinement, to enter into cummunion with the Other Self, with the Thou, with the We. The Ego longs to emerge from its prison-house in order to meet and identify itself with another Ego; but, at the same time, it must proceed warily for fear of encountering nothing but the object. Man has a sacred right to his solitude as well as to his intimate life. It would be erroneous to conceive solitude as a solipsism; on the contrary, there can be no solitude for which the existence of the Other Self and of other Egos is not synonymous with an abstract and objective world. The Ego's solitude is experienced not so much within its own existence as in the midst of others, in the midst of an *abstract* world. Absolute solitude is inconceivable; it must of necessity be relative to the existence of others and of the Other Self.

Absolute solitude would be synonymous with Hell and non-Being: as such, it can only be conceived negatively. Relative solitude implies disability and negation; but it also has a positive aspect when, transcending the common, generic and objective world, it represents a higher state of the Ego. When that occurs, the implied degree of separation is not from God and the divine world, but from the everyday social routine of a degenerate world. And this separation is a stage in man's spiritual growth.

When it is abstracted from the commonplace world of everyday life, the Ego longs for a deeper and more authentic existence. It alternates between its solitude and the everyday life of society. Kierkegaard's affirmation, that the Absolute divides rather than unites, is only true in so far as it applies to the division and union operative in everyday social life. Space and time, which determine the life of our objective world, are the real source of solitude as well as of the illusion of transcending it. Space and time divide and unite men not on the plane of authentic existence and true communion, but only on that of objective and social life. The mobility it acquires in its spatial and temporal existence is of the utmost importance to the Ego. To discard the notion of space and time is a way of escaping the fixation of solitude. But the idea of solitude invariably postulates the need and longing for communion. When man becomes aware of himself as a person and aspires to realize his personality, he has to admit firstly his inability to continue his hermetic existence and, secondly, the great difficulties assailing him in his attempt to escape from his seclusion and to identify himself with the Other Self and with the other Egos.

In a certain sense solitude is a social phenomenon, for it supposes an awareness of the Other Self. The most extreme and distressing form of solitude is that experienced in society, in the objective world. The Ego's contact with the non-Ego, with the objective world, does not solve the problem of solitude. That is, indeed, an everyday occurrence, but it only tends to increase rather than to diminish man's solitude. It is beyond dispute that no object can really alleviate man's solitude. This latter can only be overcome on the existential plane by the confrontation of the Ego with another Ego, with the Thou, with the subject. Once the Ego is abstracted from its original collective life, and has experienced the painful birth of consciousness, schism and solitude, it can no longer achieve integrity, harmony and community with others, by going back to a collective life in an objective world. It must find a way of escape from the objective world in which there is no communion or community. Solitude involves a contradiction. Thus Kierkegaard defines tragedy as a contradiction involving suffering; and comedy, as a contradiction without suffering. Human solitude postulates tragedy—an endeavour to surmount the inherent tragedy of a situation and the inability to achieve this end. Hence the even greater contradiction between the impossibility of resolving the inherent tragedy of antithesis, on the one hand, and the necessity of resolving it, on the other.

The Ego attempts to overcome its isolation in many ways: through knowledge, sexual life, love, friendship, social life, moral acts, art, and various other ways. It would be untrue to say that solitude is not to some extent alleviated in these ways; but it would be a gross exaggeration to maintain that it is thus definitely overcome; for all these ways involve objective processes, the Ego's confrontation with the object and society instead of with another Ego, with the Thou, in the depths of inner communion.

There are various forms and degrees of solitude: as an experience, it is not restricted to any one form or quality. Dispute, conflict, and even hatred are all social manifestations which often serve to suppress or to allay the sense of solitude. Their ultimate effect, however, is to increase that sense. Non-comprehension, or the Ego's unfaithful reflection in another, may also awaken a sense of solitude. The Ego experiences a profound need to be truly reflected in another, to be affirmed and confirmed by the Other Self. It aspires to be heard as well as to be seen. Narcissism is more deeply rooted in the essential Ego than is generally believed. The Ego seeks its reflection in a mirror or in water, in order to confirm its existence in the Other Self; in reality, the Ego is seeking communion with another Ego, with the Thou. It longs to find another Ego, a friend, who would identify himself with it and thus confirm it, who would admire it, listen to it; in a word, reflect it. Therein lies the deep significance of love. Narcissism, as the objective reflection of the Ego, represents its failure to achieve this; the subject remains absorbed in himself, and has no outlet or escape. The object is, in fact, the chief obstacle in the way of the subject's emergence from his inner existence and of his communion with the Other Self; it would appear, therefore, that *objectivity is an extreme form of subjectivity*.

Man's longing for knowledge is an expression of his endeavour

[71]

to overcome solitude. The pursuit of knowledge involves a longing for the Other Self, for others, an unusual expansion of the Ego and of the consciousness, and, finally, a victory over the divided world of space and time. But as long as knowledge remains objective, there can be no inducement for the Ego to emerge from the inmost recesses of its solitude. No objective form, whether it be knowledge, nature or society, is capable of reconciling the tragic contradictions inherent in the Ego; only knowledge based on communion can bring about such a reconciliation. In society, knowledge tends to acquire a social orientation and a universal character more in keeping with the realization of *communal* life than of communion.

From the ontological standpoint solitude implies a longing for God as the subject, as the Thou.[1] The divine agency is the only one capable of surmounting solitude, of making man aware of a sense of familiarity and relationship, and of disclosing a purpose commensurable with his existence. God can never be an object: when man's relationship to Him is objectified, He becomes merely an external authority. God is essentially He in Whom man can have absolute faith, He of Whom man is an inalienable part, He to Whom man can surrender himself entirely. It might be affirmed that human solitude is not a part of ontological Being, but that it only exists subjectively. Subjective existence can only be approached by a subject in close contact with the inmost depths of Being. The Ego's relationship to the world is dual. On the one hand, it involves a sense of solitude, of abstraction from the world of authentic existence; on the other, the Ego interprets world history as an inherent part of its innermost Being, and man's total experience as a part of its personal destiny.[2] Thus, at one moment, everything may appear abstract, remote; at another, everything may appear as an integral part of the Ego's own experience.

But the Ego's own experience may also be abstract. Thus society and social life are not existential, but objective and abstract; and they can offer no solution of the problem of solitude. But it is a fact that the Ego's materialization in the daily life of society is of tremendous importance to its destiny, for it demonstrates its existence on two planes—on the inner plane of authentic existence, and on the outer

[1] Cf. Martin Buber, *Ich und Du.*
[2] Cf. Berdyaev, *The Meaning of History* (Geoffrey Bles).

[72]

plane of the degraded world. The Ego's destiny in the disintegrated world must of necessity be fulfilled in social life. In a certain sense 'society' is inherent in the Ego. Carus maintains that consciousness is concerned with the particular and the individual, unconsciousness with the general and the supra-individual.[1] That is true in the sense that the whole history of the world and of society, in fact, all those elements that appear so abstract and remote to the conscious Ego, which never discloses its whole content, are latent in the depths of the unconscious Ego.

Once the Ego has been dislodged from its depths and brought into contact with objective society, it should do everything in its power to protect itself against this enemy. In his social life, while acting parts that in no way reflect his true self, man should still endeavour to preserve the integrity of his Ego. Whatever his social standing, man invariably impersonates some personage, be it a king, an aristocrat, a bourgeois, a man of the world, a father of a family, a civil servant, a revolutionary, an artist, or anyone else. The Ego of everyday social life is not the authentic Ego: that is, indeed, the fundamental theme underlying Tolstoy's literary work. For this reason, it is no easy matter to discover the authentic human Ego, to strip off its 'social' disguises.[2] In society man is invariably an actor, he lives up to the standard of conduct imposed upon him by any given social position;[3] and if he acts his part too well, he has some difficulty in rediscovering his essential Ego. Thus man's 'theatrical' Ego is but another form of objectification. Man lives simultaneously in several worlds, playing different parts and objectifying himself in a different way in each. Simmel provides a good illustration of this tendency. But we should note that man's sense of solitude is conditioned by the objectification in which he is involved and by his consequent abstraction from his true self, from his Ego. Thus the Ego would appear to postulate its own abstraction.

Romanticism, as it has manifested itself in the history of European thought, throws a great deal of light on the problem of solitude. Romanticism is, indeed, the expression of solitude, of a divorce between the objective and the subjective spheres of life; it dates from the time when the Ego became abstracted from the objective hier-

---

[1] Cf. Bernoulli, *Die Psychologie von Karl Gustav Carus.*

[2] *Vide* Carlyle, *Sartor Resartus.*   [3] Cf. Tarde, *Les lois de l'imitation.*

archical order which had until then the semblance of eternity. It is the outcome of a schism, of the soul's abstraction from an objective hierarchical order—from the *cosmos* of Saint Thomas Aquinas and Dante. The romantic Ego postulates a divorce between the subject and the object—a divorce made inevitable by the Ego's repudiation of the objective order of things. This schism had actually been brought about by the astronomical system of Copernicus and the philosophy of Descartes, as well as by the Lutheran Reformation. It supposes the development of new ideas in the scientific, philosophical, and religious spheres; the coincidence of a scientific outlook on the universe with a new philosophical interpretation of the Ego's function and with the discovery of the idea of the freedom of conscience. The 'romantic' consequences of this revolution in the human consciousness did not manifest themselves until later. When the objective world became divorced from the subjective, when it ceased to be the hierarchical cosmos, the organic centre and abode of the subject, man began to seek a way out of his solitude and isolation, to long for *familiarity* and intimacy in the subjective world. In this way he was able to develop and enrich his affective life. The romantics relied on the subjective world for their cosmic and pantheistic feelings. Their cosmos does not constitute an objective datum like the medieval cosmos of Scholastic philosophy. On the contrary, the inherent subjectivism of the romantics makes them identify man with nature; whereas Scholastic philosophy had always taken care to distinguish between the two. The romantic Ego, when confronted with a growing sense of human isolation, had sought to identify itself with the cosmos.

Although the Romantic movement may have failed to discover an adequate solution to the problems it raised, it was nevertheless an event of great importance in the emancipation of the Ego from the tyranny of the objective and social world. It liberated the Ego from the chains of a finite world, from its appointed place in a hierarchical order, and disclosed an infinite perspective. But although it did a great deal to free the Ego from the objective world, and to stimulate its creative powers and *fantasy*, it failed—and therein lies its great weakness—to make it conscious of the need to forge a personality for itself. Thus Romantic philosophy fails to be personalist; and the romantic individuality fails to be a personality. The romantic Ego tends to lose its consistency, to disintegrate in cosmic infinity. Thus the affective life, in the enjoyment perhaps for the first time of an unhampered freedom of development, overwhelms the whole content of the Ego, and subordinates knowledge to the creative imagination.

Romanticism has assumed various forms: some are excessively optimistic, and are based upon a belief in the innocence of human nature and its fusion with universal life; others, again, are extremely pessimistic in their affirmation of the Ego's solitude and of man's essentially unhappy and tragic destiny. But this type of romantic pessimism shows no awareness of the inherent sinfulness of human nature. Another aspect of Romanticism is the change of perspective it implies. In childhood, the most confined of spaces—a corner, a room, a corridor, a carriage or a tree—appear to constitute an immense and mysterious world. In the adult consciousness this feeling tends to dwindle and, eventually, to disappear. The great universe itself appears less mysterious to us than the dark corner or the corridor which had awed the infant consciousness. Romanticism gives new emphasis to the underlying mystery of the world, and thus alters our perspective. But the romantic outlook lacks the quality of permanence, it helps to disintegrate the human personality in cosmic infinity, in the ocean of affective life. But the Ego's real triumph over solitude should not be the outcome of any slavish dependence on the objective world, or of any acceptance of romantic subjectivity; the Ego must rather win a spiritual victory in the very heart of its Being; it must confirm itself as a personality capable of preserving its identity while in the process of transcending itself.

We may establish four types of relationship between the solitary Ego and the social environment: Firstly, there is the most elementary and common type: man as a social animal, unaware of solitude. In this state, the Ego is fully adapted to the social environment, and its consciousness attains a maximum degree of objectivity and sociality. This Ego has so far been spared the experience of schism or solitude. Man feels himself quite at home in the everyday social environment, in which he may even occupy an eminent position. But this type is predominantly composed of men of strong imitative instincts, of men who lack all originality of thought and are content to subsist upon a 'common' heritage, a tradition, which might well be con-

[75]

servative, liberal or revolutionary. The second type of man has no experience of solitude, but is indifferent to society. His Ego is in harmony with the social environment and collective life, but, despite its social consciousness, takes no active interest in the social life or the destiny of the people of which it is a part. This type of man is very common. Like the first type, it excludes all notion of conflict, and is most prevalent in epochs of comparative social stability. In ages of schism and revolution it naturally finds itself in great difficulty and perplexity. Thirdly, there is the type of man who is conscious of solitude, but who has no social interests. This type is either not at all or very little adapted to social life. It suffers from a divided consciousness and a lack of inner harmony. A man of this kind, although he is social to a minimum degree, is not inclined to revolt against the collective life around him, for such an action on his part would suppose both social preoccupation and emotion. Instead, he simply holds aloof, taking care to detach his spiritual life and creative instincts from the social sphere. That is usually the case of the lyrical poet, the solitary thinker, and the uprooted aesthetes. They often live their lives of detachment grouped in small societies of initiates. They are, however, ready enough to compromise with their environment when the necessities of life make it imperative. They can compromise all the more readily, because they have no fixed principles or convictions in the matter. Despite their innate indifference to political and social issues, they are prepared to be conservative or revolutionary as the occasion demands. They are neither born fighters nor innovators. And finally, there is the type of man who is conscious of both solitude and society. This may appear strange at first, since solitude is not usually compatible with sociability. This is the prophetic type everlastingly symbolized in the prophets of the Old Testament. But this type is not confined to the religious sphere; it comprehends creators, innovators, reformers and spiritual revolutionaries. The prophetic type is invariably in conflict with the social or religious collective; it is rarely in harmony with the social environment or public opinion; in fact, it has generally had to suffer persecution. The religious prophet usually has to face the hostility of the priest or pontiff, the symbol of the religious collective. Since the prophet is liable to be persecuted at any moment, he experiences the extremes of solitude. It would be difficult to maintain that the prophetic type of man was indifferent to society. The very contrary is true: the prophet is invariably preoccupied with the destiny of a people or of a society, with history, with his own personal destiny and that of the world in general. He denounces the vices of his people and of society, he judges them, but he never loses interest in their destiny. He is not concerned with his personal salvation, his own personal experiences and states, but only with the Kingdom of God and with the perfectibility of man and that of the whole universe. This prophetic type is also to be found outside the religious sphere, in that of social life, of art, and of science, which can also be prophetic in character.

The distinctions we have established between these four categories are, like most classifications, relative: their implications should therefore be grasped in a dynamic rather than a static way. The first two types are in harmony with, and the latter two are antagonistic to, their environment. It is of the utmost importance to grasp that the social revolutionary type of the third category may remain impervious to the conflicts inseparable from solitude, while being fully in harmony with his environment and possessed of a completely social consciousness. Thus the problem of solitude would appear to be rooted in the most fundamental problem of philosophy —that of the Ego, with its contingent problems of the personality, of society, of communion, and of knowledge. Ultimately, the problem of solitude involves the problem of death. To die is to experience absolute solitude, to sever all connection with the world. Death implies the disruption of a whole sphere of Being, the termination of all relationships and contacts—in a word, complete isolation. If the ultimate mystery of death could be shared, if it could still comprehend a relationship with the Other Self and with others, we would not call that state death; for death is the severance of all relationship, the end of all communion, the attainment of absolute solitude. Death does effectively put an end to man's intercourse with the objective world.

It is still problematical whether that solitude is final and everlasting; or whether it is but a moment in the destiny of man, of the world, and of God. Man's purpose in life should be to establish such relationships and contacts with other men, with the universe and with God, as would help him to transcend the absolute solitude of death. Or more exactly, we must not think of death as of the Ego's complete annihilation. That is, indeed, a most difficult thing to achieve. We ought rather to envisage death as the moment of the Ego's complete severance and abstraction from the divine world. Death is paradoxical because this severance and abstraction are the outcome of the Ego's materialization in the degraded and objective world of everyday social life. The relationships evolved in this state lead irrevocably to death. We are thus confronted with the problem of the Ego's relation to the object, on the one hand, and to the Thou, on the other; in brief, we have to consider the problem of communication between consciousnesses.

THE EGO, THE THOU, THE WE AND THE IT—THE EGO AND THE OBJECT—COMMUNICATION BETWEEN CONSCIOUSNESSES

In his notable book, *Ich und Du,* Martin Buber, the Jewish religious philosopher, has established a fundamental distinction between the *Ichsein,* the *Dusein,* and the *Essein*—the Ego, the Thou, and the It. According to him, the primary relationship between the Ego and the Thou is one between man and God. This relationship is dialogical or dialectic. The Ego and the Thou are thus confronted one with another. For the Ego, the Thou is not an object or a *thing*. But when the Thou is transformed into object, it becomes the *Essein,* the It. In terms of my own philosophy, this *Essein* or It is the outcome of objectifying processes which obscure the Thou and make a confrontation with it impossible. The third person is either the Thou or the It. The Thou is never an object in relation to the Ego. But nothing is immune from objectifying processes which manifest themselves even in religious life. The object is synonymous with the It, the *Es* of Buber. As they are progressively objectified, nature and society are equally liable to be transformed into the It; but as soon as we are confronted with a Thou, the objective world gives place to the existential. Buber very rightly maintains that the Ego has no real existence outside of its relationship with the Other Self or the Thou; but he envisages the relationship between the Ego and the Thou as one uniquely between man and God, as expounded in the Bible. His investigations do not extend to the relationship between human consciousnesses, between the Ego and the Thou, between two human beings, or to the diverse relationships implied in the multiple life of mankind. Nor does he consider the problem of social and human metaphysics, that of the We.

But the existence of the We cannot be ignored, and its relationship to the Ego, the Thou, and the It must be considered. That the

We can be transformed into the It by the operation of socializing or objectifying processes is evident from the history of the Oecumenical Church as a social institution. The objectified We is synonymous with the social collective imposed on the Ego from without; but it has also another aspect, that of community and communion with other people, a communion wherein each person is not an It but a Thou. Society is the It, not the We; its objectification transforms each of its members into an object. In such a state, they are neighbours, not fellow-beings or friends, for a friend can never be an object. A society is made up of nations, classes, various social strata, parties, citizens, comrades, superiors, but never of the Ego and the Thou, for the social We is objective, an abstraction from the concrete person.

But there exists another kind of communion between human consciousnesses, based upon their participation in the We, which does not represent the It, the object, or any exterior datum in relation to the Ego. The We is a qualitative content immanent in the Ego, for every Ego is invariably related not only to the Thou but also to multiple mankind. The pure ontological idea of the Church is founded upon such a relationship; the effect of objectification is to empty the Church of its existential content. Existence is revealed in the Thou and the We, as well as in the Ego, but never in the object. Freud, in spite of a philosophical naïveté sometimes bordering on materialism, draws a distinction between the Ego and the Self.[1] According to him, man has within him an impersonal foundation, the Self, which may dominate the Ego. Heidegger's One (*Das Man*) in a sense corresponds to Buber's *Essein*, which, though it coincides with what I term the objective world, does not sum up the whole of the social problem. Heidegger's world of *Dasein*, of the *determined Being*, is the *Mitwelt*, the *coexistent world*. But unlike Jaspers, Heidegger does not consider or develop the problem of metaphysical sociology. Even if we assume that the We, as well as the Thou and the It, are immediate data,[2] it remains none the less true that the Ego is the anterior, primitive entity; I cannot say, 'I', without thereby affirming and postulating the Thou and the We. In this light, sociability is a constituent property of the Ego's in-

[1] Cf. Freud, *Essais de Psycho-analyse*, III, Le Moi et le soi.
[2] Cf. S. Fraux, *Les Fondements spirituels de la Société*.

timate existence. We must draw a clear distinction between the Thou and the We, on the one hand, and the non-Ego on the other, that is, between the existential and the objective. The Thou is but another Ego, whose particular content is the We. The non-Ego is invariably hostile and opposed to the Ego. At the most, the Ego may find a measure of reciprocity in the non-Ego, the other half of Being, but this reciprocity is not that of the multiplicity of other men, because the non-Ego, as an object, excludes the Ego.

Until recently philosophy has not paid sufficient attention to the relationship between the Ego, the Thou, and the We; it has been content, rather, to investigate the reality of the *Other* Ego, and the means of apprehending it. But that reality, and our ability to apprehend it, may be questioned. According to the old theory, our perception is limited to the physical aspects of another's presence, and the soul's existence can only be inferred by analogy. This theory is completely erroneous and should be discarded forthwith. As a matter of fact, our knowledge of another's body is very limited. We can only perceive it superficially and can have no idea of what goes on within it; but our knowledge of other people's psychic life is infinitely greater; we are better able to grasp it and to penetrate more immediately into it. The intuition of another Ego's mental life is an undeniable phenomenon liable to occur only when a Being or an existence is envisaged as an Ego or a Thou, and not as an object. When confronted with an object, the Ego remains solitary and self-sufficient; but in the presence of another Ego, which is also a Thou, it emerges from its solitude in an endeavour to achieve communion. *The intuition of another Ego's spiritual life is equivalent to communion with it.*

The vision of another person's countenance, the expression of his eyes, can often be a spiritual revelation. The eyes, the gestures, the words—all these are infinitely more eloquent of a man's soul than of his body. We can derive our knowledge and perception of another person's life not only from what that person may reveal, but also from what he may attempt to conceal of himself. This latter method of acquiring knowledge about other people has been much abused of late as a result of the discovery of the unconscious. Freudian psycho-analysis undoubtedly demonstrates the possibility of apprehending the psychic as distinct from the physiological life, for the

Freudian definition of the *libido* attributes to psychic life a spiritual rather than an organic origin. No less erroneous is the belief that the analytical method is the only one which can throw any real light on man's inner life or, in other words, on his true Ego. Any attempt to make the Ego an *object* of knowledge only helps to isolate it in its own depths. There does exist, however, an immediate way of apprehending another's spiritual life—it is the affective, sympathetic, *erotic* way. But the mystery of the Ego persists, and resists all attempts to solve it. It would be an error, however, to conclude that it is totally impossible to apprehend an Ego's spiritual life.[1]

Too little attention has been paid so far to the problem of communication between consciousnesses. And yet it is one of the fundamental problems of philosophy.[2] *A clear distinction should be made between communication and participation.* Participation is something *real*; it is the penetration of primary reality. Communication, on the other hand, is for the most part symbolic; it makes use of symbolism or of exterior signs to denote an interior reality. The symbolism of communication is that part of the inner life which transpires into the objective and disintegrated world. This symbolism, which helps to establish communication as well as to indicate a state of disintegration, permeates both our knowledge and art. Our knowledge of other people's inner life is acquired mostly through signs and symbols—a mode of communication which prevents any real solution of the mystery of existence by helping to conceal the underlying state of disintegration. Therefore the value of such communication can only be symbolic. That is true of customs and usages, of imitation, politeness and amiability, in fact, of all the modes of communication which constitute social life, but do not suppose any degree of real communion between persons. Thus pecuniary relations, which are objective to a degree, are governed by symbols of an essentially conventional character. But the Ego cannot be content to communicate with others only through the medium of society and State, of institutions and conventional signs. It aspires to communion with others, to achieve authentic existence by transcending itself. Conventional modes of communication submerge the

[1] Cf. Max Picard's interesting work *Das Menschengesicht.*

[2] The problem is considered by Jaspers in the second volume of his *Philosophie: Existenzerhellung.*

[82]

Ego in the objective world, whereas its longing for communion points the way to the extra-natural world of authentic existence. The symbolism of communication varies in proportion to the degree of objectification.

Communion implies reciprocity: it can never be one-sided; there can be no communion in unrequited love. In a state of communion both the Ego and the Thou are active, whereas there can be no reciprocity in the symbolism of objective communication. In order to achieve communion on an existential plane, it is necessary for the Ego to commune with another Ego, which must also be a Thou, an active Thou. The Ego remains isolated as long as it can only communicate with the object; its solitude can only be vanquished by the communion of personalities, of the Ego and the Thou, in the innermost depths of the We. The human consciousness has a social foundation since it postulates the existence of other men and their relationships, that of human fraternity. But, as is often the case, the human consciousness may prove to be an obstacle rather than a means to authentic communion, when it assumes a social form based upon symbolic communication. Man's consciousness as expressed in its social forms is at the mercy of everyday collective life. Mystic ecstasy, on the other hand, can overcome all the barriers and obstacles in the way of the communion of consciousnesses. It may happen that, in order to quench this longing for communion, man may endeavour to satisfy his consciousness by overriding the barriers and norms of everyday sociality by the force of his creative originality and supra personal ecstasy. Personal and original thought, which is nearest to the primary source of life, does not invalidate community or communion, but only its subjection to everyday sociality, to objective society. *Personal thought is not an indictment of community, but of general principles.* Jaspers very rightly maintains that no Ego can exist without communication with others, without a dialectical conflict. The conversion of the world into a mere subject of knowledge necessarily involves objectification, that is, a system of communications based upon outward authority and general principles, which exclude the hope of achieving an inner community.

The process of objectification implies rationalization. But the Ego is most truly reflected in the affective life, wherein knowledge is least objectified and the emotions have not been socialized to the extent of obscuring the Ego's inner life. The intimate communion of one Ego with another gives rise to an affective kind of knowledge. It is an error to think that communion can only be a human relationship, that it is the attribute solely of *human friendship*. It is common to the animal, vegetable and mineral worlds, which all enjoy an inner life of their own. Like Saint Francis one may commune with various manifestations of nature, such as the ocean, the mountains, the forest, the fields, the rivers. A striking example of this type of affective communion is furnished by man's relationship to that true friend, the dog. This relationship reconciles man with objective, alien nature, and thus transforms the object into the subject, into a familiar and friendly relationship. This relationship has a real metaphysical value, inasmuch as the resistance of the object is overcome and authentic existence is achieved.

In his theory of Narcissism, Freud identifies the Ego with the object of its *libido*. Narcissism is the sign of a divided Ego, of an Ego that becomes its own object, a part of the objective world. This division can only be overcome when the Ego seeks to identify itself with some other Ego. Narcissism is a phenomenon frequently encountered in the sphere of knowledge. According to Freud, man's deepest instinct is death. Freud is apparently unaware of the mystery of communion, of the Ego's passage through the Thou and the We. The sexual instinct does not in itself lead to communion, to identification with another Ego. It contains a demonic and destructive element, and tends to make us slaves of the objective world. Hence Freud's contention, that the instinct of death is next in importance to the sexual instinct, is proof that he knows no other.

Esctatic communion on the supra-personal plane, the suppression and the negation of the personality, are ways of escaping from the disrupting and constraining influence of everyday life and of solving the problem of solitude. In the ancient cults, in the Dionysian cult for example, the mask symbolized man's victory over solitude, his participation in the divine mystery. But that does not solve the problem of communication between one Ego or personality and another. The solution lies in love, in erotic and friendly love; for love is intimately related to the personality and is the means by which the Ego emerges from its self-sufficiency in quest of another Ego as opposed to another impersonal or collective Self. But the

Ego is only an embryonic personality; to become one in reality, it must commune with the Thou and the We. It is this communion of personalities longing to be reflected in one another which confirms the personality. The Ego's reserve is an expression of its solitude and isolation. It is its way of protecting itself from the social and objective world. The Ego's essential need is communion with the Thou, but it is in constant danger of being confronted with the object. As a result, it adopts a defensive attitude to shield its consciousness from the brutal contact with things. Thus, although its enforced solitude is a phase in the personality's development towards self-consciousness, it is a phase that must be transcended. But objectification, the building up of an impersonal world, is not a means of achieving this end. We shall therefore have to consider more particularly the problem of the personality.

CHAPTER III

SOLITUDE AND KNOWLEDGE—TRANSCENDENCE— KNOWLEDGE AND COMMUNION—SOLITUDE AND SEXUALITY—SOLITUDE AND RELIGION

The pursuit of knowledge is undoubtedly one of the ways of overcoming solitude; it compels us to abandon our self-centred isolation, and situates us in another space and time where we are brought in contact with the Other Self. It is an escape from solitude, a way of getting to know the other Ego, the divine world. Through it man emerges from his seclusion, ceasing to live uniquely for and in himself. Nor can the social aspect of knowledge be ignored, the fact that it helps to establish communication between men. All its attributes, its communal logic as well as its logical apparatus, its concepts, language, norms and laws, are all manifestly social.[1] Language is the most powerful instrument for constituting society and establishing communication between men; but it is also related to thought and the elaboration of notions indispensable to an intellectual community between men. Names may have the effect of social magic.[2] The practical results of knowledge depend on the degree of community between men, on their social groupings, on their assiduous co-operation—in a word, on the manner in which they combat solitude. All these facts raise the complex question of the relation between knowledge and solitude.

But it does not follow that, because knowledge is social and helps to foster communication between men, it achieves complete communion or transcends solitude. Social and objective are synonymous terms; but the object obscures the underlying mystery of existence, the apprehension of which alone can bring about communion and the triumph over solitude. The problem of knowledge may there-

[1] A great deal of information on this point may be found in the works of sociologists like Durkheim and Levy-Bruhl.

[2] Gundolf has a lot to say about the magic content of the name Caesar. Cf. his work *Caesar*.

fore be approached in two ways: from the standpoint of objective society, and from that of communion, of inner existence and of familiarity with the Thou. Only the latter approach is capable of overcoming solitude. There are two aspects of knowledge: one comprehends the relationship between the knowing subject and Being; the other includes the relationships between the knowing subject and other Egos, the multiple world of men and society. In the first case, the problem of solitude is resolved by the participation of the knowing subject in the mystery of existence; in the second, the social processes only succeed in objectifying man, in blunting the Ego's sensibility and consciousness, that is, in merely achieving a superficial result.

A real communion, a real triumph over solitude, can only occur when the Ego identifies itself with the Thou, as in the case of love and friendship. The same is equally true of knowledge. The Ego's contact with an object or society is not sufficient to banish solitude; it must commune with the Thou and the We. Because knowledge is invariably concerned with the *general*, the abstract and the universal, it tends to overlook the individual, the singular and the personal. But when the union of the Ego with the Thou is also a communion, its universal results acquire a greater validity precisely because they are based upon the individual, the singular and the personal. The true affirmation of individuality is to be found in what is universal and concrete rather than in what is general and abstract. Solitude can, indeed, be overcome when the universal and the general dominate the particular and the singular, but only at the cost of the total suppression of the Ego and, consequently, of the Thou. But in terms of Existential philosophy, knowledge is primarily concerned with the Ego and the Thou; it is essentially personalist. In fact, it is important not to submerge solitude in impersonal generality, but to transcend it by the agency of the personality. By emancipating itself from the yoke of society, of a logical and social community, knowledge could make its thought supra-logical.

To triumph over solitude is to *transcend* the Ego in the sphere of intellectual or emotional life. But the Ego has two different ways of transcending itself: by identifying itself with an object or a general principle and by entering into communion with the Thou. There is certainly a positive value in the act by which the Ego emerges into

[87]

the objective world in the process of instituting society or of elabo-rating the general principles and concepts indispensable to communication, but the world of this transcendence is a degraded, disrupted and circumscribed world. The light of the *Logos* is reflected even in the general principle inherent in objective knowledge, but this reflection is a mere glimmer in an otherwise opaque world in which the human Ego is but a slave. Thus the problem of knowledge is rich in contradictions and antinomies, as is shown in its contingent problems of communion, of time and of the personality. Objective processes succeed in achieving a merely superficial reconciliation of these contradictions; in reality, the progress of objective knowledge only helps to multiply them. The idea of God is the only solution capable of effectively resolving these often intolerable contradictions. God, according to the masterly definition of Nicolas of Cusa, is precisely the *coincidentia oppositorum*.

The nature of knowledge is conjugal; it supposes a duality; it can-not be the exclusive product either of the object or of the peculiar agency of the subject. For this reason, solitude can be overcome only by a cognitive act based upon true love; for there can be no real union with the general, but only with another Ego, with the Thou. The conjugal essence of knowledge is theandric; it has both a human and a divine aspect. The effect of objective processes is to eliminate both these elements, and to substitute in their place impersonal and general principles. The inherent difficulty of knowledge consists in transcending this impersonal and general state, so as to achieve the conjugal union of personalities. But it may happen that the Ego, in its pursuit of knowledge, fails to triumph over solitude, and is obliged to seek union in other ways. The knowledge I have in mind comprehends not merely the academic learning of savants and philo-sophers, but also the experience of everyday communal life, which is especially open to the tyranny of general principles and of social imitation.

Sex is one of the chief causes of human solitude. Man is a sexual being, that is, half a being,[1] divided and incomplete, aspiring to be complete. Sex brings about a profound division of the Ego, which is by nature bisexual, both male and female, androgynous. Thus man's endeavour to overcome solitude through communion is

[1] The original Russian word for *sex* means both *sex* and *half*.

[88]

primarily an endeavour to overcome the isolation caused by sex, to achieve reunion in sexual integrity. Its very existence implies separation, want, longing, and the desire to identify oneself with another. But the physical union of the sexes, which puts an end to sexual desire, is not in itself sufficient to banish solitude. Indeed, it may only intensify man's sense of solitude. Another result of sexual union may also help to precipitate the Ego into the objective world, because sex is a natural phenomenon situated in the objective world. Marriage and the family are its social consequences. As a biological and social phenomenon, sexuality is objective, and therefore incapable of completely allaying solitude. The biological union of the sexes and the institution of the family may, indeed, to a certain degree allay and diminish the sense of solitude, but they are unable permanently to vanquish it. There is also a demoniac element in the inhibitions as well as the manifestations of sex. This demonism makes sexuality a deadly and destructive thing.

Love and friendship are man's only hope of triumphing over solitude. Love is, indeed, the best way of achieving this end, for it brings the Ego in contact with the Other Self, with another Ego in which it is truly reflected. This is the communion of one personality with another. An impersonal love, which is not concentrated on any individual image, does not deserve to be called love. Rozanov spoke of this kind of love as 'glass love'. It is very likely a perverted form of Christian love. Friendship, too, has a personalist and erotic foundation. The personality and love are intimately related, for *love transforms the Ego into a personality*. Only love can effect that complete fusion with another being which transcends solitude. The pursuit of knowledge cannot achieve this unless it be inspired by love. The disintegrating and demoniac aspect of sexual life may also manifest itself in love; for the materialization of human existence in the objective world tends to make love a tragic and mortal experience. The objective world, that of biology and of society, cannot suffer the idea of authentic love and its disdain for both natural and social laws. This love is only concerned with the extra-natural order wherein solitude is eliminated. And that accounts for its intimate relationship with death.

We are once more confronted with duality. Sexual communication may take place within the framework of society and of social

G [89]

institutions, but it is powerless to achieve true communion or to vanquish solitude. The sexes may also unite in an extra-social community of love, and thus really overcome solitude. In the social and objective world, however, sexual union is the prelude to a tragic destiny, to a mysterious alliance with death. Dualism is insurmountable within the limits of the natural world. It comprehends, however, the principle of transcendence without which there can be no achievement of the authentic life or escape from the limitations of a circumscribed world. Transcendence is the very essence of love. Man is impelled towards it by his poignant sense of solitude in an ice-bound world of objects and by his need of communion with the Other Self. But such is the metaphysical mystery inherent in sexuality that even the very height of passion, a love as overwhelming as that of Tristan and Iseult, fails to banish completely the sense of sexual solitude and longing. A demoniac element of hostility persists between the lovers. Thus the ultimate triumph over solitude may be regarded as the realization of the image of a perfect androgyne. But this in its turn implies the transfiguration of nature. It is therefore true to say that the problem of solitude is most acutely felt in the sphere of sexuality.

Communism eliminates this problem by identifying the Ego with the social collective, and by substituting a collective consciousness for the personal one. The Ego's existence is definitely objectified in the process of social construction. Hence the importance which communism assigns to eugenics, to the mechanism and technical aspects of sex, in short, to the negation of personal love. Such a system of farmyard breeding is intended to stifle sexual longing and its inherent sense of solitude. The *erotic* aspect of human life is sacrificed to the economic and technical aspects. The same tendency is apparent in the German racial doctrine, which attempts to solve objectively an essentially extra-social and existential problem. But there is nothing novel in this: the same negation of personal love and the same conception of sexual life are to be found in the teachings of certain doctors of the Church. Sexual life has two fundamental aspects: firstly, it forms a part of the Ego's inner existence, as well as of that of the human destiny and of the human personality; but it remains in constant tragic conflict with the hostile objective world of society and of the family. Secondly, it is based on a racial urge which impels it to assume objective and social forms. That is also true of the Will to power which, though intimately related to man's innermost destiny, has the effect of plunging him into the social and objective world. The rule of power or of might only extends to the objective world and is incapable of triumphing over solitude. Thus the destiny of a Caesar or a Napoleon is perforce a tragic one.

Religion implies a relationship: it may be defined as an attempt to overcome solitude, to release the Ego from its seclusion, to achieve community and intimacy. Its very essence associates it with the mystery of Being, with Being itself. But only God is capable of overcoming solitude: religion only implies a relationship, and, as such, can only be secondary and transitory. Transcendence and plenitude, as well as the purpose of existence, are only manifest in God. There is a tendency to overlook the fact that God is the primary consideration, that religion can prove an obstacle to man's communication with God.[1] Man's relations to God as historically manifest in religion, are not free from a certain element of objectification. When religion becomes a mere social and objective manifestation, the sense of solitude fails to be ontologically transcended; if that sense is diminished, it is due to the Ego's immersion in the objective world and society, even though that world be called the Church. Transcendence can only take place if the relationship between the Ego and the divine world is rooted in the inner life, in the Church-community as opposed to the Church-society. It follows that our affirmation of an inherent duality, of any opposition between the Spirit and nature, between freedom and necessity, between existence, or primary life, and objectivity, holds equally true of religion as well as of knowledge and sexual life. Religion is most certainly a social institution, something secondary and objective, a projection of the inner life into the natural world. But religion can also be Revelation, the voice and incarnation of God, a primary manifestation independent of the social and objective world.[2] Even then it does not follow that religion is but an individual event and the privilege of a certain number of isolated souls. On the contrary,

[1] Karl Barth notes this very clearly, and that is the positive aspect of his theology. He is more convincing in his *Römerbrief* than in his dogmatic philosophy.

[2] Cf. the already quoted work of Bergson, wherein he expresses an idea analogous to the one underlying my book, *The Destiny of Man*.

[91]

religion not only binds and unites man to God, but it is also the essential bond between man and his fellow-beings; it is both community and communion. This union is consummated on an extranatural plane wherein each man, as well as God Himself, is a Thou, and not an object. The mystery of Christianity consists in the Ego's transcendence in Christ, the Divine Man, in His theandric nature, in the *Corpus Christi*. The triumph over solitude involves more than a formal adherence to the Christian faith or membership of the Church, more than a merely superficial transcendence. A purely social Christianity of this type can never give rise to anything more than a conventional, symbolic, and unreal conception of love. True love then, as the very summit of life, remains the only effective way of transcending solitude.

A degree of objectification is implied in any purely formal adherence to the Christian confession. The penetration of an object does not liberate the Ego from its sense of solitude, because no real union can be ontologically effected between it and the object. A distressing and painful sense of solitude can therefore be experienced in the very heart of the Church itself. Man may feel himself infinitely more alone in the midst of his co-religionists than in the midst of men of totally different beliefs and persuasions; his relations to them may be of an exclusively objective kind. Such a state of affairs is extremely distressing and tragic, and demonstrates the fundamental duality of religious life. An increase of spirituality may only aggravate the sense of solitude, for it may be accompanied by a total rupture of man's social relationships in the objective world. But there is no way of avoiding such ruptures, however painful they may be, once man has embarked upon the path of spiritual progress; for solitude can only be transcended on the spiritual plane, only in mystic experience, wherein all things participate in the Ego and the Ego participates in all things.[1] This path is diametrically opposed to that of objectification, which effects communication only between extrinsic and abstract things. Christian symbolism is itself an indication that its means of communication and its relations are too often purely conventional, verbal and *rhetorical*. In fact, the whole life of society is based upon an imitative 'rhetoric'.

But, on the other hand, there is also the endeavour to realize the

[1] Cf. Berdyaev, *Freedom and the Spirit.*

[92]

true, spiritual and mystic life. Mysticism itself is not always exempt from conventional rhetoric or from the objective processes of every-day society. But we are here concerned with its essential nature. In its depths human existence participates in the spiritual extra-natural order. Only in these depths, of which mysticism is perhaps the symbol, is solitude really vanquished. Objectification may have the effect of allaying the anguish inseparable from solitude; in identifying the Ego with an object or a society it tends to banish the immediate sense of solitude; but such identification, even when it occurs in the religious sphere, is in no sense a true victory over solitude. It is a state preceding the nascent consciousness of solitude as a revelation of the essential nature of Being. Therein lies the whole complexity of the problem of solitude as manifest in the various spheres of knowledge, of sexual, social and religious life. A review of the evils attendant upon human solitude involves the chief problems of Existential philosophy, regarded as the philosophy of human destiny. The evil of time is another and no less distressing problem intimately associated with it.

FOURTH MEDITATION

THE EVIL OF TIME. CHANGE AND ETERNITY

CHAPTER I

THE PARADOX OF TIME; ITS DUAL SIGNIFICANCE— THE NON-EXISTENCE OF THE PAST—THE TRANSFIG- URATION OF TIME—TIME AND ANXIETY—TIME AND CREATIVE ACTIVITY

The problem of time is the fundamental problem of human existence. It is no accident that Bergson and Heidegger, the two most considerable philosophers of present-day Europe, have made this problem the pivot of their philosophies.[1] Existential philo-sophy envisages the problem of time in a different way from the Mathematical and Naturalist philosophies. It interprets the problem of time as that of human destiny. It is but indirectly interested in such concepts as 'potential and actual infinity', 'the infinite', 'the indefinite', 'the transfinite', elaborated by Mathematical philosophy.[2] Human destiny is realized in time, under the aegis of time. Naïve realism errs when it conceives time as a framework comprehending and determining the mutations of existence. In reality, change is not brought about by time, but time by change. Time exists because there is activity, because there is creative action, because there is an incessant passage from non-Being to Being. But this creative activity is discontinuous and disintegrated; it has no roots in eternity. Time is the product of *changing* realities, beings, existences. Time can therefore be transcended. The degraded time of our world is the outcome of the Fall that occurred in the depths of existence. It is the product of objective processes, of an objective, disintegrated and determined world. It would be naïve to maintain that there is noth-ing extra-temporal. Time is only a state of things. But there also exists an extra-temporal state. Time has a dual significance for human

[1] Cf. Bergson, *Essai sur les données immédiates de la Conscience*, and Heidegger, *Sein und Zeit*.

[2] Cf. Bertrand Russell, *Introduction to Mathematical Philosophy*, and Brunschvicg, *Les Étapes de la Philosophie mathématique*.

[97]

existence: on the one hand, it is the outcome of creative activity; on the other, as the product of disruption and disintegration, it is synonymous with fear and anxiety. Bergson claims to have discovered in duration the positive meaning of time. Heidegger, on the contrary, is concerned with the negative aspect of time, with its resultant anxiety.

Time may be subjective or objective. It would appear to be the product of an objective process experienced by the subject. Time is objective in another sense than that ascribed to it by naïve realism. Objectivity is the product of objective processes and not, as is commonly believed, a given external reality. That is also true of time. Heidegger makes time the ontological foundation of the *Dasein*, that is, of the 'materialized existence' or, according to my terminology, of objectification. He maintains that anxiety has the effect of making Being temporal. Thus time is a sense of anxiety. But that is only one of the aspects of the temporal process which is the outcome not only of anxiety and fear, but also of the change engendered by creative activity. In the process of time non-Being becomes Being. In its essentials, Heidegger's philosophy is the philosophy of the *Dasein* rather than that of Existence, the philosophy of anxiety rather than that of creation; and for this reason it is only concerned with one aspect of time. Man's outlook on the future is determined not only by anxiety and fear, but also by creative activity and hope. Therein lies the dual significance of time. The sense of time is based not only on fear but also on creative activity. Neither Bergson nor Heidegger attaches sufficient importance to this duality, which is based upon the impossibility of admitting either the static or the dynamic aspect of human nature. To admit stasis would be to deny the process of eternal renewal; to admit dynamism would be to deny the eternal foundations of human nature. Thus duality is inherent in the very structure of the personality defined as the union of the mutable and the immutable.

Time implies two kinds of change; change through the ascension of life and change through death. In that portion of itself which we call the future, time is both fear and hope, anguish and joy, anxiety and deliverance. The Hindoo philosophers, as well as Parmenides, the Platonic philosophers, and Eckhardt, all affirmed that time was unreal and illusory, vain and derogatory to eternity. But Christian

[98]

philosophy, which was also the foundation of historical dynamism,[1] has always maintained the ontological value of time as a manifestation of purpose. That, too, is the conception of dynamic Evolutionism. Some schools of thought consider that change is merely an illusion, and they ascribe an ontological value only to the immutable and the static. Others maintain that change is itself a reality, that creative action and activity introduce innovation and benefits of a positive kind, and also add to the significance of Being. An authentic philosophy of human existence can only subscribe to the second point of view.

In his *Confessions*, Saint Augustine propounds some remarkable ideas about time.[2] He is perfectly aware of its paradoxical and illusive nature. According to him, time resolves itself into the past, present and future. But it then transpires that the past is no more, that the future is not yet, and that the constant disintegration of the present into both the past and future makes it evanescent. We must therefore conclude that there are three different kinds of time: the present of things past, the present of things present, and the present of things future. Time is a kind of disintegrated eternity whose fragments, past, present and future, are equally elusive. Man's destiny is fulfilled in this decomposed eternity, in this terrifying reality of time, in this mirage of the past, present and future. This accounts for its essential instability. Bergson, on the other hand, establishes a distinction between time and duration. He maintains that duration is the source of authentic existence. At the same time, he has a perfect grasp of the duality underlying the world. He calls the world of degraded existence, the objective world, spatial. His spatial world is fundamentally the same as Heidegger's 'temporal' world. Disintegrated eternity degenerates into objective time, wherein the past, present and future are all disassociated. Under these circumstances, it is essential to investigate further how the past, present and future are related to the Ego's destiny, and what significance may be ascribed to this fluctuating existence. In the first place we must ask ourselves the question: has the past ever really existed, and if so, how does that affect our own existence?

The past is no more. Its real and existential content has been ab-

---

[1] Cf. Berdyaev, *The Meaning of History*.
[2] Saint Augustine, *Confessions,* Book IX.

[99]

sorbed into the present. The past and future, in so far as they still persist, form a part of the present. The whole history of our life, as well as that of mankind in general, is incorporated in our present, and only exists by virtue of this. That is, indeed, the fundamental paradox of time, that my destiny is fulfilled within a time divided up into the past and future; that time itself is the fulfilment of my destiny in spite of the fact that the past and future only exist within my present. There must therefore be two different kinds of past: the past which has been and is no more; and the past which still persists as an integral part of our present. The past which lives on in the memory of the present is quite a different past, a transfigured past, which our creative acts have helped to reintegrate into our present. Memory is not merely the conservation or the resurrection of the past; it implies creative innovation and the creative trans-figuration of the past. The paradox of time is further demonstrated in the fact that the past has never really existed as the past. What did exist in the past was then actually the present, another present; the past, as such, only exists in the present of to-day. But the past and the present have an absolutely distinct existence. The present past is distinct from the past regarded from the standpoint of the present. There are two ways of considering the past, that is, things and beings that have perished: the conservative standpoint, which harks back to the past, implies faith in tradition; and the creative and transfiguring vision which integrates the past in the future and in eternity, and resuscitates dead things and beings. Only the second approach is in harmony with the present which is inherent in the past; the first merely reflects the actual present which is always becoming the past.

The problem of the past and future, that of their mutual relations, has a dual aspect: on the one hand, the problem is how to do away with the sinful, evil and painful past; on the other, how to per-petuate past beauty, goodness and love? This approach to the past is very similar to the way in which we approach the present. We endeavour to preserve our cherished present, and regret to see it leave us or die. We endeavour to forget that part of the present which is painful and ugly. The present we most cherish and value, should be everlasting, exempt from any future conversion into the past; for the effect of the future is precisely to make the present past.

Such is the fatal relationship between the past and the future. Time is an evil, a mortal disease, exuding a fatal nostalgia. The passage of time strikes man's heart with despair, and fills his gaze with sadness. It is significant that such a notable writer as Proust should have chosen the pursuit of fleeting time, the artistic recreation of the past in the memory, as the fundamental theme of his work. Towards the end of his creative career Proust believed that he had recovered and reconstituted lost time, and in the second volume of his *Time Regained* he attains to an almost religious pathos. The problem of time has, indeed, become an essential part of philosophy as well as of art. It has always been an essential part of religion, and particularly of Christianity. The mysteries of penitence and absolution, of death and the Resurrection, of the ultimate goal and the Apocalypse, are fundamentally those of time—of the mystery of the past, the present and the future.[1]

Wherein lies the root of time's evil and its accompanying nostalgia? It lies in the fact that man finds it impossible to experience the present as a complete and joyful whole, as a part of eternity, or to shake off, even while enjoying the present instant, the dread of the past and of the future, and of their nostalgia. It is not our lot to experience the joy of the instant as we might experience the fullness of eternity, for this joy is invariably tempered by time's impetuous flight. As a particle of fleeting time, the instant is alive with all the distress and cruelty of time eternal in the process of being divided into the past and the future. But the instant, because it also participates in eternity, has another quality. The instability and transience of all things gives rise to a deep sense of melancholy and fear in face of past and future events. This sense of melancholy and fear can only be overcome by the exercise of creative activity in the present and the refusal to envisage the future in terms of fatality or determination.

Thus we fulfil our destiny and realize our personality in time; but we abhor time as a synonym of disintegration and death. Carus speaks of the Promethean *foreseeing* and of the Epimethean *mnemonic* principles. But the Promethean principle is not merely a *foreseeing*

[1] Cf. Eberhard Griesebach, *Gegenwart. Eine Kritische Ethik.* Under the influence of Kierkegaard and dialectic theology, he propounds the problem of the present in a different way from myself.

principle, it is above all an heroic one, endowed with a creative activity capable of triumphing over both nostalgia and fear, as well as over the fear of the future, envisaged as necessity and predetermination. Memory is undoubtedly man's most profound ontological principle, the one that cements and preserves the unity of his personality. But man cannot live in a degraded world without feeling the need for oblivion, the need to forget many things. Integral memory, that of the past and the future, would be too heavy a burden for man. In that sense oblivion is a deliverance and an alleviation. Man is constantly endeavouring to forget himself, to forget both the past and the future. He actually succeeds in forgetting himself only for the briefest moments; but the need he experiences of oblivion attests to the mortal evil of time.

There are men who live essentially in the past, the future, or eternity. The sphere of men's temporal lives is generally restricted; only a few men ever attain to a vision of eternity that is also a triumph over the evil of time. Prophets behold the future because they can transcend time and judge it on the spiritual plane of eternity. For them, time will change its dimensions and become eternity. It is a common error to identify the past with eternity. As a matter of fact, there is an element of eternity in the past, just as there is an element of it in our present and future. But the past contains much that is perishable and transient, in fact, more evil than eternity. The conservative consciousness, which tends to idealize the past, may mistake these transient elements for the semblance of eternity. But it would be an error to deny that the past participates in eternity, or to affirm that eternity is only revealed in the future. Neither the past nor the future, as fragments of disintegrated time, have any prerogative over eternity. It is the instant of communion with eternity which we should consider sacred—and not the social or objective figments of the past and the future. The future has the advantage of freedom, of active creation, as the only way of overcoming the notion of determinism invariably associated with the past. But freedom, too, should be related to the past in such a way as to make possible the inversion of time.[1] The religious consciousness envisages this problem as that of the Resurrection. It is the problem pro-

---

[1] *Vide* V. Mouravieff's curious book, *La Conquête du Temps*, which shows the influence of Feodorov's ideas.

pounded in Feodorov's *The Philosophy of Communal Work*, wherein he demonstrates that the mortal nature of time can be vanquished.

Time Regained is not merely an attempt to interpret the past or the future; it represents a real victory over time's evil. Time thus reintegrated becomes eternity. Creative activity therefore should concentrate not on the future with its implied fear, anxiety and determinism, but on eternity. Its motion is inverse to time's acceleration, which is the product of technology and of the nostalgia inseparable from a passively emotional acceptance of mortal time. It is, on the contrary, a sign of spiritual victory.

On the ontological plane there is no past or present, but only an incessantly created present. Our interpretation of time is profoundly transformed when we envisage it from the creative standpoint. Whereas Heidegger affirms that anxiety helps to make Being temporal, it is evident that creative activity, on the other hand, can liberate Being from the tyranny of time. The creative act itself transcends time, but its actual material results have their place in one or other of time's divisions—in the past, the present or the future. Time, and all it symbolizes, is but the objective expression of the total experience contained in the extra-temporal instant. The future may be the materialization of the anxiety consequent upon the degradation of the world; or it may be the materialization of the creative act whose concrete results form part of the degraded world. The temporal and spatial materialization of existence is an objective process; for the objective world is essentially temporal and spatial. Time assumes a very different significance when viewed from the standpoint of man's inner existence. The temporal character of man's destiny in the degraded world is but a secondary feature; for time is governed by human destiny, and all the changes and events involved in it. The theological doctrine of the Creation is not a revelation of primary truth, because it is an attempt to be objective. It is, rather, the expression of naïve realism. In reality, the Fall did not take place in time, but rather time was the outcome of the Fall. Actually, the notion of the Creation is an intellectual antinomy: the world cannot be eternal; nor can its origins be purely temporal.

This antinomy is invariably the result of objectification. We tend to conceive Creation from the standpoint of the object, of the objective world and of time. But in the light of the inner existence,

[103]

of the spirit, everything is transfigured, and Creation is no longer dependent on any category of time. Creation is eternal, whereas time is a degraded state of the human destiny. It would be erroneous, however, to envisage time merely in the light of human degradation; for time is likewise the outcome of dynamism, of creative activity, although it is only their material result. In reality, time belongs to the inner plane of existence; and objective thought is merely the exteriorization of inner events. The real tragedy of human existence lies in the fact that an act committed in the present can determine our whole future in all time, perhaps in eternity. That is, indeed, a terrifying prospect—a terrifying materialization of an act which has essentially no such aim in view. It involves the problem of the future materialization of man's destiny. In this connection, we must consider the problem of vows—those of fidelity, of monasticism, of marriage, of the orders of chivalry, of secret societies. We shall have occasion to return to this.

Man's highest dream and greatest achievement are to experience the plenitude of a given instant. All the wisdom of Goethe, the whole import of his life, are the result of this faculty to experience fully, to discover the divine element in the minutest particle of universal life. In this way, he was able to triumph over time's evil. Time is anterior to space; the latter, indeed, postulates the former. The scientific theory, which affirms that time is a fourth dimension of space, has no metaphysical value. Its application is restricted to the objective world. It may, indeed, be affirmed that a fourth dimension is indispensable for the accomplishment of events. But from the standpoint of Existential philosophy, time is anterior to space; time generates those events and acts which occur in the depths of extranatural Being. The primary act does not suppose either time or space, but itself engenders both time and space. And yet the primary act of human existence excludes both determination and causality, which are the outcome of objective processes. There is no trace of determination or causality in the creative subject.

As we shall see hereafter, death is the ultimate aspect of the problem of time. Death is inseparable from time, and occurs within its framework. The fear of the future is above all the fear of death. Death is an event within life itself; it is the term of life. But death is only the ultimate result of life's materialization. It occurs in time, within the objective world, but not within the subject or his inner existence, wherein it is merely an instant of his eternal life. The past with its sequence of extinct generations is dead only when we regard it as an object, when we ourselves are merely material phenomena. Memory is the manifest sign of the inner life, of the fact that no Being or existence can be exclusively a part of the natural world. To be conscious of tradition is to wage a battle against the empire of time, to commune with the mystery of history. But a mere revival of the past for its own sake is not an achievement of eternity or a triumph over death, that sovereign ruler of the natural world. On the contrary, such a revival would only consolidate the power of time. Thus Nietzsche's vision of the eternal renewal is one of the most terrifying visions of time's everlasting sway over authentic Being.

TIME AND KNOWLEDGE—REMEMBRANCE—TIME, MOVEMENT AND CHANGE—THE ACCELERATION OF TIME AND TECHNOLOGY

Knowledge and time are intimately related. Through knowledge man is enabled to escape from any given time. Plato had taught that knowledge was remembrance, or, in other words, that it was a victory over the empire of time. History, which is the science of the non-existent, of what has no connection with reality, illustrates this relationship between knowledge and time. History, indeed, whether it studies man or the universe, is the science of what has once been, but is no more. The objective reality of historical science is based upon the idea of the former existence of the past. The fact that certain elements of the past still persist in the present, and are part of it, is what determines the possibility of historical knowledge. But the surviving monuments of the past have lost all their original associations. Let us affirm once more that the past has never existed in the past. The ontologically real experience of the past is based upon memory and remembrance, which alone ontologically resist the ravages of time. Memory alone can apprehend the inner mystery of the past; it is the temporal agent of eternity. The Ego's consciousness is likewise related to memory,[1] which reveals, in the metaphysical depths of that consciousness, the whole history of the past as an aspect of man's personal experience concealed in the heart of his Being. History, like everything else, has two aspects: on the one hand, it is an objective process in so far as it investigates the past as an object and is, consequently, relegated like nature to the objective world; on the other hand, it is a spiritual event in the inner sphere of existence. As a spiritual event, history can only be apprehended by means of the ontological memory and active communion with the past. To achieve this result, man must apprehend

---

[1] Bergson goes into this question very thoroughly.

the past as a part of his own existence, of his own pre-historical spiritual existence. The past thus becomes an integral constituent of his present, and man is enabled to overcome temporal disintegration.

Knowledge is remembrance when it involves a reality not communicable by immediate sensible experience, that is, when it involves an experience outside this disintegrated time we call the present. Our spiritual activity is based upon remembrance, because present experience can never be more than a fraction of our knowledge. And thus, since memory is the primary constituent of the personality and of the Ego, the human consciousness in the process of remembrance tends to absorb the whole history of the world in the depths of the existential Ego; and that history, if it is truly the Ego's history, should be inherent in its memory. Knowledge cannot be the product of ignorance, nor can it be engendered by an evolutionary process. It implies an *a priori* awareness, the remembrance of an ancient wisdom. Knowledge is communion with the Logos. But that is only one of its aspects, namely, the Platonic. It also has a creative aspect. At this point we shall have to consider again the problem of time. Knowledge is also an event in Being, a transformation, an illumination of Being. Therefore, the knowledge of the past is paradoxical because it is the knowledge of the non-existent, the past never having been an event in Being. But the future has no more reality than the past, since it may fail to materialize. But if the inner remembrance can enable man to apprehend the non-existent past, the prophetic spirit should likewise be able to reveal the non-existent future. We must distinguish, however, between prophecy and scientific prevision. This latter occurs only when the future is considered, like the past, as something static, objective and entirely determined. Prophecy, on the other hand, interpreted in the widest sense, represents the mystery of transcended time, the mystery of man's emancipation from its yoke, the mystery of his conquest of the eternal present and of his communion with it. It reveals the mystery of existence, that of the future as an integral part of this existence. The eternal present thus revealed is not a static present, but one in the process of incessant creation outside the frontiers of disintegrated time.

Parmenides is the original source of all doctrines affirming the static nature of Being and the illusion of all dynamism and change.

This conception was incorporated in Christian theology. But it fails to explain the enigma of knowledge. Actually, however, knowledge is synonymous with innovation in Being; it represents dynamism, change, creation; it demonstrates the impossibility of static Being. It is an event in Being, a change occurring within it. The victory over time implied in knowledge, as in other spiritual acts, in no way postulates the attainment of a static and immutable timelessness. In reality, our world is an incomplete world still in the process of creation. From the standpoint of man's inner existence, the world is always creating itself rather than evolving. The evolutionary changes in the world are but a secondary process implying determinism and materialization. The inner life is governed exclusively by the creative impulse, freedom and spiritual activity, rather than by evolution, determinism and natural causality. Evolution is a temporal phenomenon, obeying temporal laws. But the primary spiritual acts engender time itself. There are changes which are not determined by time, but which, on the contrary, determine time. Thus time and its determined evolution are but the materialization or objectification of the creative changes occurring in the inmost depths of existence. In a sense, time is a lapse from eternity, though it remains inwardly present in eternity. Dynamism and change therefore have their genesis in eternity. And thus the world was created, but not determined, in eternity. Determinism is only a feature of the objective and secondary world, which is governed by the past, present and future, of a disintegrated time, that is, by what has no real existence. In this world, we tend to conceive eternity itself as a temporal infinity.

The objective world is therefore a world of mathematical time, of mathematical infinity. This measurable time, recorded by clock and calendar, is very different from that of man's inner destiny. But human destiny is also expressed in the objective world, where it becomes the slave of mathematical and divisible time. Indeed, only the spiritual life can be free from numerical time. The duality of time is most clearly revealed in the instant. The instant is significant in two absolutely different ways: firstly, the instant is a minute fraction of time, mathematically small but divisible in its turn, interposed in the stream of time between the past and the future; secondly, there is the instant of extra-numerical, indivisible time, the instant which cannot be disintegrated into the past and the future, the instant of the eternal present, indivisible and integrally part of eternity. Such is Kierkegaard's *Augenblick*. To-day, in a century of technology and speed, the problem of time has become particularly acute. Time has undergone a frenzied acceleration to which the rhythm of human life must respond. No instant has intrinsic value or plenitude, but must rapidly yield to the succeeding instant. Each instant is but a means to the succeeding instant. Each instant is infinitely divisible and, therefore, has no validity. The era of technology is entirely orientated towards the future—a future wholly determined by the development of time.[1] Swept away by the torrent of time, the Ego has no leisure to affirm itself as the free creator of the future. These present-day phenomena are the sign of a new age. The speed consequent upon the increasing mechanization of life has had a deadly effect on the human Ego, and has sapped its foundations of unity and consistence. The advent of machinery and the mechanization of life have led to an extreme objectification of human existence, to its materialization in a strange, inhuman and frigid world. And though this world is the work of man, it is essentially anti-human. The effect of high speed has been to disintegrate the human Ego into minute fractions, into a succession of instants in disintegrated time. The Ego's unity and integrity are related to the unity and integrity of the indivisible present, of the instant in its plenitude, of the instant that is more than merely a means to a succeeding instant, of the instant that is also a communion with eternity. The Ego is essentially active and creative. But it also supposes contemplation, without which there can be no concentration, deeper significance or integrity; without which the Ego can be diverted from its primary activity and objectified or abstracted from its own authentic existence. The Ego, in its endeavour to realize its personality, has as much need of contemplation as of creative activity. The Ego expresses itself in movement, activity and creative innovation; but to realize itself completely it must also be able to contemplate, to investigate deeply, to concentrate, to emancipate itself from time, and, finally, to identify itself with the instant. Without the power of contemplation the Ego would be in danger of being swallowed up in the infinite universe. The objective Ego becomes a part of the

[1] Cf. Berdyaev, *Man and the Machine*.

[109]

infinite universe and its multiple movement, and it is everywhere at the mercy of infinity (which is not eternity). Nineteenth-century thinkers saw in the Ego's dependence upon cosmic infinity a proof of determinism. To-day, scientists as well as philosophers interpret this phenomenon in a different way. They incline to find in this permanent action of cosmic infinity, in this multiple cosmic movement, a source of indetermination. At the present time science favours a statistical interpretation of the natural laws and is prepared to admit the agency of chance.[1] In the light of this theory, human destiny is the product of chance rather than of natural determination. But the theory of indeterminism advanced by modern physics, which has accepted the free agency of atoms, does not help to alleviate the lot of human destiny. Indeterminism, however, may prove to be less fatal to man than determinism. The theory of relativity introduced a momentous change in the physical conception of the world and discredited the old scientific theory of determinism. But it only helped to confirm the deplorable state of human existence in the objective world. The temporal evil afflicting the degraded world finds its confirmation in all the scientific and physico-mathematical theories of time. As life becomes more technical and mechanical, so the evil of time is increasingly virulent. The full implications of this, however, can only be grasped from within by means of Existential philosophy.

[1] Cf. Emile Borel, *Le Hasard*.

CHAPTER III

TIME AND DESTINY—TIME, FREEDOM AND DETERMINISM—TIME AND FINALITY—TIME AND INFINITY

The idea of time is inseparable from destiny; and it is, indeed, as time that we experience our destiny. The problem of time is ultimately eschatological. Christian philosophy, unlike the philosophies of India and Greece, endows time with a positive significance. To be conscious of time is to be conscious of history, of one's own history and of universal history. Existence is a part of eternity, but, as Jaspers very rightly remarks, it derives its significance from time. Thus time only becomes intelligible in the light of human destiny. By concentrating time in a single point, and by extending in this way the effects of each particular act to the whole of eternity, Christianity has prodigiously intensified time. The doctrine of the Reincarnation, on the contrary, is based upon a diffuse conception of time—of a time that is answerable for itself. Intensive time holds out the promise of an immediate admission to eternity, that is, of admission within time to those events whose significance is eternal as well as temporal. But surely it would be most unjust to assume responsibility for acts committed in an instant of time, even if that instant were to correspond with the span of our life. In a detached instant of time man could never attain to the plenitude of experience and knowledge, the breadth of vision, which would make him consciously assume responsibility for eternity. Man could not assume for ages to come the burden of what had occurred in a single instant of time, unless that instant represented not merely a fraction of time but also a participation in eternity, unless that instant had been abstracted from time. It is beyond man's powers to apprehend eternity in an instant of time, because eternity is extra-temporal.

At this juncture the problem assumes a different aspect. To represent man's destiny, his eschatology, from the standpoint of time merging into eternity, where the totality of times, eternity itself, will be answerable for a single instant of time, is to objectify human destiny, to uproot it from its depths and to materialize it. In this light eschatology becomes a natural phenomenon in accordance with the traditional interpretation of eschatological doctrine. The attainment of eternity postulates time as an integral part of eternity rather than as something objective and infinite, as something completely abstracted from extra-temporal eternity. This reintegration of time is accomplished precisely in that instant, which breaks the temporal succession of other instants and becomes, instead, a qualitatively original and indivisible whole. Such an experience of the instant cannot be objectified for the benefit of the future or of an infinite time. There are two possible ways of experiencing time: one is to experience the present without reflecting about the future and eternity; the other is to identify the present with eternity. The first attitude is really based upon oblivion, upon a lapse of memory, considered as the essence of the personality. Living in the present is another way of defining it. Moreover, this instant of oblivion may be devoid of any particular value; it may denote, for example, that a man is in a state of intoxication or is obsessed by some passion, neither of which states is at all likely to lead to eternity. The second attitude, on the other hand, does overcome time's evil and lead us towards eternity. In this case, the instant is not that of oblivion, but, on the contrary, that of a particular plenitude, representing man's entire life illuminated by memory rather than by any fraction of his isolated life. Thus the spirit can triumph over the fear and terror of the future. The evil experienced in an instant of time does not constitute a plenary experience, nor does it have any bearing on the plenitude of human destiny; it is invariably an incomplete experience isolating the part from the whole. But this particularism and this isolation are precisely the reason why human destiny can have no definite solution. The evil-engendering instant remains the slave of time, and fails to attain to eternity even when the latter is a synonym of Hell. The fatal character of the past and future is the result of our tendency to objectify time and to represent both the past and the future as objects to which we should be subordinate. But, of course, the past and future have no ontological existence when they are objectified in this way. In reality, both the past and the future are subjective, and are only parts of man's inner existence. The traditional doctrine of Heaven and Hell is entirely the product of objective processes.

The past has all the appearance of having been determined; and that is the only sense in which we can speak of determinism. But this involves objectification—the exteriorization of inner events. And inner acts, when they are objectified, appear to constitute a necessary chain of events, a determined evolution. But it would be rash to affirm that the future is in any way determined. The future can be experienced as freedom or destiny; but destiny also involves freedom and is therefore not a synonym of determinism. As I have already pointed out, the quantum and the discontinuity theories of modern physics propound indeterminism and the negation of the natural laws as they were understood in the nineteenth century.[1] To-day chance plays a preponderant part; and chance cannot, of course, be fitted into any determined sequence. Chance is infinitely nearer to freedom than the natural laws.[2] The Ego is a free agent or a destiny when it experiences chance. A chance meeting, which may have a lasting effect on a man's destiny, may be interpreted as a result of freedom or fate, or again as a manifestation of a supreme *raison d'être,* as a sign of another world, but never as a result of determinism. Here is a relationship between time and freedom never suspected by evolutionary determinism. Time exists because change exists. But change invariably occurs in the inmost depths of Being, and only objectification can make it appear to be the result of a determined sequence, of an evolution or involution. But is change a betrayal of eternity? That opinion is widely shared—especially by those who are determined to preserve their faith in the immutable order of nature and society. But no such order exists outside of an objective phase which may disintegrate and dissolve under the pressure of creative acts. Change therefore cannot affect eternity or be a betrayal of it. It is not related to eternal time, but only to past time, which creates the illusion of eternity. The transfiguration of the world, the dawn of a new Heaven and Earth, is the greatest and most drastic of all changes. This presentiment is a proof that eternity does not co-exist with the temporal order.

[1] Cf. the collection of essays by Louis de Broglie, Vialleton, etc., entitled *Continu et Discontinu,* published as one of the volumes of *Les Cahiers de la Nouvelle Journée.*

[2] Cf. E. Boutroux, *De la Contingence des Lois de la Nature.*

The personality stands in a paradoxical relationship to time. The personality is synonymous with change and with perpetual creation, and yet it is at the same time immutable. Thus, on the one hand, it is temporal in so far as it realizes itself in time, but, on the other, it eschews time, like every other form of materialization, as a danger to its existence. The mutations undergone by the personality in the course of its existence suppose its transcendence, an act by which it transcends itself. The experience of the transcendental in the inner depths of existence is an act of transcending, and not an objective transcendence imposed from without. Outward transcendence can only occur on the secondary and objective plane. The transcendental can only be conceived as a mystery with which the Ego communes by means of an immanent process. This communion constitutes a transcendental act which penetrates into the inmost depths of eternity, and which has need of time only in the objective world. We are thus led to consider the problem of the Apocalypse as a problem of time.

The difficulties in the way of understanding and interpreting the Apocalypse are due to the fact that, like every eschatology, it is a revelation of the paradoxical nature of time. It symbolizes the clash of time and eternity, and the insurmountable contradictions resulting therefrom. There are two ways of interpreting the Apocalypse: firstly, from the standpoint of the future, of time; and secondly, from that of eternity and of the supra-temporal. When we consider the problem of finality, that of the end of the world and of man, we may well ask ourselves whether that end is related to time, that is, to the future; or whether it is inherent in the things themselves, in the destiny of the world and of man, outside the notion of time and of the future. We may formulate the paradox of time inherent in the Apocalypse as follows: the end of time, of all time, the achievement of timelessness, will take place in time, in the future. Thus, the symbolic revelation of the Apocalypse concerns both the natural and the extra-natural world; it is both historical and extra-historical, both temporal and supra-temporal or eternal. It is impossible to describe the passage from time to eternity, the end of all time, for we tend to think of the timeless world in terms of that portion of our disintegrated time which we call the future. Thus we think of a timeless world as an achievement of the future. But this conception involves a contradiction; for timelessness implies the abolition of any kind of future, of its possibility even. The future that precedes timelessness is still our objective temporal future, and this makes it difficult for us to conceive the possibility of its cessation at any stage or of its becoming the supra-temporal. Indeed, this is not an event that can take place in the future, in time, but only on another plane. The future is invariably envisaged from the objective plane of existence, but timelessness cannot be envisaged from such a standpoint. Timelessness would mean the end of the objective world, the attainment of the inner spiritual life.

The traditions and dogmas of Christian eschatology are full of insurmountable difficulties. Nor do they throw any light on human destiny in its passage from death to the end of the world. How are we to reconcile man's individual death and resurrection with those of the universe? That is the fundamental paradox of time, the paradox of the future, of the objective future. What we call the eternal life is not the same as the future life. Heidegger affirms that 'anxiety' is the ruling motive of man's temporal Being; his category of the *Dasein* is founded upon the finite nature of time, upon the mortality of Being, the *Sein-zum-Tode*. Thus death, as he defines it, is 'Being-orientated-towards-the-end'. Heidegger has apparently no other solution of existence. That accounts, of course, for the profound pessimism of his philosophy, in which the idea of eternity plays no part. The same is true of Bergson, in spite of the more optimistic character of his philosophy; his *duration* is not eternity.[1]

The idea of eternity is opposed to the nightmare of both finite and infinite time. Time, as we have already observed, is the relation between one reality and another; it also supposes a change in those realities as well as in their relationships. Finality is the synonym of death. It is, however, related to time and space. But the fact that finality is death is a proof of time's infinity. For if we were to postulate an end to time, we would be involved in a contradiction, since without infinite time there could be no end to Being, there could be no such thing as death. There are two kinds of infinity: one made up of quantity and sum; the other, of quality. The problem of infinity may therefore be approached in these two ways. Quantitative infinity is mortal and affirms an infinite time. Qualitative infinity

[1] *Vide* A. Eggenspieler's recent book *Durée et Instant*.

triumphs over death, and affirms the finite character of time and the healing of time's evil. Certain philosophers, like Renouvier, maintain that everything finite is perfect, while everything infinite is imperfect. That, indeed, was the contention of ancient philosophy, correct enough in terms of quantitative infinity, but erroneous in terms of qualitative infinity. Eternity is precisely this qualitative infinity, and it alone offers a solution of the paradox of time. Eternity is situated in the extra-natural world, away from the world of quantitative infinity and mathematically divisible time. The inner life is not governed by numerical time. The intensity of the inner life modifies the nature of time and endows it with a new dimension. But this is a point upon which each person must endeavour to enlighten himself by his own personal experience. The happy proverbially take no heed of the hours. On the other hand, those who suffer may have to endure an eternity of infernal torture. Every one knows how time accelerates or slows down according to the intensity of life and the nature of the events that make up human existence. The mathematical character of time may lose all significance, and human existence may liberate itself from the tyranny of the clock and calendar. If we are liable to count the hours, we are most likely unhappy. Creative inspiration can likewise dispense with numerical time. It is always the sign of eternity's irruption into time, whose course it regulates. The non-eternal or what has no eternal origin or goal can have no validity; it is doomed to perish, and the future only holds out to it the promise of death, of finality in time as opposed to the *finale* of time. A time that does not participate directly in eternity is a degraded time; but time is also an instant of eternity, and that is its sole justification. The paradox of time is therefore an ambiguous one, since it is based upon contradiction.

Man is tormented by two fundamental problems which illumine all others: the problem of the origin and the foundation; and that of the future, the issue and the goal. Both these problems are indissolubly related to the notion of time, and they bear witness to the fact that time is really man's inner destiny. But the beginning and the end, the origin and the goal, extend beyond time. The temporality of human existence is the outcome of a degraded state, though its original nature is extra-temporal. But the temporal course of human nature is only confined to its middle stage during which it is assailed by the mortal evil of time. For this reason time is full of nostalgia for the past as well as for the future. The fear of the future is to some extent the fear of death, which in its turn is the fear of damnation. This fear is invariably inspired by the temporal aspect of human destiny, by time's lack of finality, that is, by the fear of infinite materialization. What we fear in the future is not the act but the object, not what we can create but what we may have to endure. The future may inspire us with either hope or fear. Every man has to live his inner Apocalypse, which is based on the fundamental paradox of time and eternity, of the finite and the infinite. This Apocalypse reveals the ways in which we can realize our personality. Thus we are confronted with the ultimate problem of the personality.

FIFTH MEDITATION

THE PERSONALITY, SOCIETY AND
COMMUNION

CHAPTER I

THE EGO AND THE PERSONALITY—THE INDIVIDUAL AND THE PERSONALITY—THE PERSONALITY AND THE THING—THE PERSONALITY AND THE OBJECT

The fundamental problem of Existential philosophy is that of the personality.[1] I am an Ego before I become a personality. The Ego is primary and undifferentiated; it does not postulate a doctrine of the personality. The Ego is postulated *ab initio*; the personality is propounded. The Ego's purpose is to realize its personality, and this involves it in an incessant struggle. The consciousness of the personality and the endeavour to realize it are fraught with pain. Many would rather renounce their personality than endure the suffering which its realization involves. The idea of Hell—impersonal Being has no notion of it—is connected with this human endeavour to preserve and develop the personality. The personality is not the same thing as the *individual*,[2] which is a natural biological category comprehending not only the animal and the plant, but also the stone, the glass, the pencil. The personality is a spiritual category; it is the spirit manifesting itself in nature. The personality is the direct expression of the impact of the spirit on man's physical and psychical nature. A brilliant individual may have no personality. Men of great talent and individuality may be impersonal and unable to furnish the effort required to realize their personality. We may say of a man that he lacks personality, but we cannot deny him individuality. Maine de Biran and Ravaisson both maintained that the personality was intimately connected with human endeavour,

[1] This book was already going to print when I came across N. Hartmann's new work, *Das Problem des geistigen Geist*. Its contents are interesting. But my definition of the object differs fundamentally from Hartmann's. Thus, for example, I do not admit the existence of an objective spirit; the spirit can never be objective.

[2] From the Thomist standpoint, Maritain distinguishes the individual, as a part, from the personality, as a whole. Cf. his *Du Régime temporel et de la Liberté*.

which, in its turn, is inseparable from suffering. This endeavour is free from any exterior determination. The personality, like God, is extra-natural; and since it is the image and likeness of God, it is intimately related to Him. It postulates the supra-personal: it could not exist but for a Higher Power, a supra-personal content. The personality is above all an 'axiological' category: it is the manifestation of an existential purpose. The individual, on the other hand, does not necessarily postulate such a purpose or contribute any value to life.

The personality is not in any sense substantial. To conceive it as such would be to adopt a naturalist, non-existential position. Max Scheller defines the personality more correctly as the union of our acts and their potentialities.[1] The personality may also be defined as a complex unity, made up of the spirit, the soul, and the body. An abstract spiritual unity, lacking in diversity and complexity, does not constitute a personality. The personality is totalitarian, for it integrates the spirit, the soul and the body. The body is an integral part of the personality; it has its place not only in the material, but also in the cognitive sphere.

The personality is also the symbol of human integrity, of permanent values, of a constant and unique form created in the midst of incessant flux. In this way, the individual identity of the body is preserved despite the total renewal and change in its material composition. The personality postulates further the existence of a dark, violent, and irrational principle, the soul's capacity to experience powerful emotions; it also postulates the soul's ultimate and everlasting triumph over this irrational principle. But although it is rooted in the unconscious, the personality implies an acute self-consciousness, a consciousness of its unity in the midst of change. It is sensitive to all the currents of social and cosmic life and open to a variety of experience, but it takes care not to lose its identity in society or in the cosmos. Personalism is opposed to either social or cosmic pantheism. The human personality has nevertheless a material content and foundation. It cannot be a part of any social or cosmic whole;[2] it has an autonomous validity which prevents its

[1] Max Scheller, *Der Formalismus in der Ethik und die materiale Werthetik.*

[2] *Vide* Levy-Bruhl's excellent work, *L'Ame Primitive,* with reference to the relations of the individual and the collective in primitive societies.

being converted into a means. It is an axiom of an ethical kind—
the sort of axiom that enabled Kant to express an eternal truth in a
purely formal manner. From the Naturalist standpoint, the personality is only a minute part of nature; from the Sociological standpoint, it is only a minute part of society. But from the Existential
standpoint, from the standpoint of Spiritual philosophy, the personality cannot be conceived as anything particular and individual
as opposed to anything general and universal. This opposition, so
characteristic of the natural and the social life, is no longer applicable
to the human personality. The supra-personal helps to build up the
personality, while the general constitutes the foundation of the particular without transforming the personality into a means. Therein
lies the mystery of the personality—a mystery based on the coexistence of contraries. The error of universalism, which would
make the personality an organic part of the world, lies in its in-
organic conception of the personality. Parallel theories of society
are all equally impersonalist, and attribute to the personality a merely
organic function. To understand the personality, we must approach
the relationship between the part and the whole not from the
naturalist, but from the *axiological* standpoint. The personality is
never a part but always a whole, never a datum of the external
world but always a datum of the inner world of existence. It is not
an object, and has no place in the abstract objective world. It is not
of this world: when confronted with the personality, I am in the
presence of a Thou. It is not an object, a thing, or a substance; nor is
it an objectified form of psychic life—the object of psychology.
Thus, the triumph of the personality will mean the annihilation of
the objective world. The personality has an 'image', a concrete
form; but that image is the expression of a whole, never of a part.
The personality is the realization within the natural individual of
his *idea*, of the divine purpose concerning him. It therefore supposes
creative action and the conquest of self. The personality is spirit
and, as such, it is opposed to the thing, to the world of things, to
the world of natural phenomena. It reveals the world of men, the
world of living beings, who are concrete by virtue of their relationship and of their existential communion. The personality postulates
discontinuity and thus excludes monism. Being a conscience, it is
not determined by any psycho-physical structure; it has its roots in

another order. The personality is a biography, one and unique, an 'history'. Existence is invariably 'historical'.

Although W. Stern's philosophy is fundamentally rationalist, it is personalist in its opposition of the *personality* and the *thing* (*Person und Sache*)[1]—a distinction which replaces the traditional one between *spirit* and *matter*. Stern defines the personality as that existential something capable of constituting, despite its multiplicity, *a unity possessed of originality and value*, and of forming, despite the multiplicity of its particular functions, *a unity endowed with independence and finality*. This distinction is valid from the physical as well as from the psychic standpoint. According to Stern, the essential quality of the personality is its *unitas multiplex*. The personality is an integral whole, not a sum of parts. It is an end in itself, whereas the thing is but a means to an end. The faculty of being a free agent is the essential characteristic of the personality. The *entelechy* is that which can set itself a goal; the *mechanism* is merely an inverted entelechy. Stern elaborates a whole hierarchy of overlapping personalities. He even ventures to admit the 'nation' into this hierarchy.[2] Therein lies the error of his system: the nation is an individual, but not a personal category. But Stern has undeniably been able to discern a number of peculiar characteristics which distinguish the personality from the thing. But his definition, like the majority of definitions, is rationalist, and his personalist doctrine therefore cannot claim to be strictly existential. The essence of the personality invariably eludes him. His personalism is not specifically human, for his category of the personality, comprehends objects and collectives wherein man is no longer the centre of interest. Another most important property distinguishes the personality from the thing, that of being able to experience joy and suffering. It is endowed with a sensibility wanting in the suprapersonal realities: the sense of a unique and indivisible destiny is its essential constituent. That is the absolutely irrational aspect of the personality's existence, whereas the freedom of choice constitutes its

[1] A brief account of this doctrine may be found in *Grundgedanken der personalistischen Philosophie*. Stern's principal work is entitled: *Person und Sache. System der philosophischen Weltanschauung*.

[2] Cf. G. Gurvitch, *L'Idée de Droit Social*. Gurvitch propounds an anti-individualist doctrine wherein there is no hierarchical subordination. He is obviously indebted to Krause and Proudhon.

rational aspect. The essential character of the personality lies not so much in its teleology, as in its power to achieve an antinomian blend of freedom with predestination when working out a troubled destiny.

As a matter of curiosity, we may note that the Latin word 'persona' signifies a 'mask' and has theatrical associations. The personality is essentially a mask. Man employs it not only to disclose himself to the world, but also to defend himself from its importunity. Thus acting and 'representation' symbolize not only man's desire to play a part in life, but also his need to protect himself from the surrounding world, to preserve his identity in the depths of his Being.[1] The theatrical instinct has a dual significance. On the one hand, it is the result of man's social condition, of his life in the midst of a multitude of fellow-men among whom he aspires to act a part, to occupy a position. The theatrical instinct is fundamentally a social one. On the other hand, it symbolizes the Ego's identification with another Ego, its reincarnation, the personality's masquerade. This is invariably a sign that the personality has failed to overcome its solitude in society, in the natural intercourse between men; that man is ever lastingly solitary beneath his disguise. The Dionysiac orgies endeavoured to overcome solitude by annihilating the personality. Solitude, indeed, can be overcome only in communion, only in the knowledge of the spiritual world, and not in the world of social frequentation, of the multitude and its objective relationships. When authentic community is achieved, the personality is strictly itself, and obeys the dictates of its own nature; instead of reincarnating itself in another Ego, it unites with the Thou while at the same time preserving its own identity. But when the personality is plunged into the midst of the multitude, into the midst of the objective world, it invariably aspires to play an assumed rôle, to reincarnate itself in others, and thereby ceases to be a personality, becoming merely a person or an individual. A social position generally involves acting a part, assuming a mask, incarnating a personage imposed from without. But on the existential plane, on the extra-natural and extra-social plane, the personality insists on being itself; and man seeks to find his own reflection in another human countenance, in the Thou. This longing to be truly reflected is inherent in the personality and its 'image'. This latter seeks a faithful mirror. In a cer-

[1] Cf. the work already quoted by Evreinoff.

[125]

tain sense it implies narcissism. Love, the lover's image, is such a faithful mirror, the desired communion. There is something distressing about photography, which does not mirror the loving countenance, but only objectifies it and thus robs it of its true expression.

Nothing is more significant, nothing reflects more the mystery of existence, than the human image.[1] It is intimately related to the problem of the personality. Like a beam of light from the mysterious world of human existence, which reflects also the divine world, it invariably breaks the spell of the objective world. Thanks to it, the personality can enter into communion with other personalities. There can be no comparison between the perception of a countenance and that of a physical phenomenon; it is a communion with the soul and the spirit. It is evidence that man is an integral being, as opposed to one divided in flesh and spirit, in body and soul. It symbolizes the victory of the spirit over the resistance of matter. That is, indeed, Bergson's definition of the body. But it applies above all to the human image. The expression of the eyes is not an object, a physical phenomenon; it is the pure manifestation of existence, the apparition of the spirit in a concrete form. An object only serves human ends: the human image exists only for communion. As Stern has very rightly observed, the personality's Being is 'meta-psycho-physical'.

The Ego may be able to realize itself, to become a personality. But this realization is invariably accompanied by a self-limitation, a free subordination of the self to the supra-personal, the creation of supra-personal values, the escape from self and the penetration of other selves. The Ego may also remain egocentric, absorbed in itself, incapable of identifying itself with others. But egocentrism is fatal to the development of the personality; it is the greatest obstacle in the way of its realization. The free development of the personality precludes self-interest, and must be based entirely on its aspiration to commune with the Thou and the We. The egocentric man is completely devoid of personality, of all sense of reality; his world is one of phantasms, illusions and mirages. The personality, on the other hand, supposes a sense of realities and the ability to comprehend them. Extreme individualism leads to the negation of the per-

[1] Cf. M. Picard, *Das Menschengesicht*.

sonality. From the metaphysical standpoint, the personality is social because it feels the need of communicating with others. Personalist ethics are likewise directed against egocentricity,[1] which endangers the preservation of man's identity, unity and personality. Egocentricity may, indeed, bring about the destruction of that identity, and may disaggregate it into distinct instants unconnected by any thread of memory. The egocentric man may have no memory, he may lack the very essence of the personality's identity and unity. Memory is a spiritual phenomenon, it is a spiritual endeavour to preserve man's being from the disintegrating influence of time. Time's evil effect is to disintegrate the personality's unity into independent fractions. But this evil has no power to create an integral personality in its own image. Thus an element of goodness is always preserved. The struggle to preserve the personality is also one directed against megalomania and madness. To abandon this struggle may lead to mental derangement and the loss of all sense of reality. Hysterical women are generally unbalanced and obsessed by their Ego—a state of mind most destructive to the personality. A divided personality is the outcome of egocentricity. Solipsism, although no more than an intellectual exercise in philosophy, is synonymous, in psychology, with the negation of the personality. If the Ego is self-sufficient, the question of the personality does not arise. There are various forms of egoism; some are commonplace and trivial, others exalted and idealist. Egoistic idealism is not at all propitious to the development of the personality. Philosophical idealism, as expressed in early nineteenth-century German philosophy, leads directly to impersonalism. That is especially evident in Fichte's theory of the Ego, stripped of all human attributes. The pernicious effects of this impersonalism are particularly manifest in the Hegelian doctrine of the State.

Monism in any form is incompatible with personalism. The very idea of the personality implies a dualism. The monist doctrine of the universal Ego has nothing in common with the doctrine of the personality. Personalism, however, is to be met with but rarely in philosophy;[2] rationalistic systems of thought have invariably been monis-

[1] Cf. Berdyaev, *The Destiny of Man.*

[2] Father Laberthonnière maintained that personalism was the only Christian philosophy. Personalist philosophy originates with Maine de Biran.

[127]

tic. The enigma of the personality has proved most baffling for philosophical thought as the enigma most dependent upon Revelation for its solution. Unlike the individual, the personality is not a natural phenomenon; nor is it a datum of the natural or the objective world. The personality is the image and likeness of God, and that is its sole claim to existence; it appertains to the spiritual order and reveals itself in the destiny of existence. The anthropomorphic aspects of knowledge are, in spite of their frequent deformation, intimately bound up with the destiny of the personality, with the immediate semblance of the divine and human images. And that is the strongest evidence of the real distinction between the personality and egocentricity.

According to Christianity, the ontological kernel of the human personality is situated in the heart, which represents not a differentiated element of human nature, but an integral whole. It also represents the essence of man's philosophical knowledge. Intelligence alone cannot constitute such a kernel of the human personality. Moreover, both contemporary psychology and anthropology reject the classical division of human nature into the intellectual, the volitional, and the affective elements. The heart is not any of these distinct elements; it is the seat of wisdom and the organ of the moral conscience, which is the supreme organ of all evaluation.

It is essential to distinguish between the two senses in which the notion of the personality may be interpreted. The Being of the personality is distinct and original, and has no affinity to any other Being. The idea underlying the personality is aristocratic in the sense that it suffers no promiscuity, and that it implies selection and a qualitative standard. Thus the problem of the personality in general becomes that of the personality endowed with a *particular* vocation, with a goal in life, and with creative power to achieve it. The propagation of democratic forms in a given society may help to undermine the personality, to bring about a general levelling, to reduce all men to an average standard, and, finally, to produce 'impersonal' personalities. On the basis of this affirmation, we might be tempted to conclude that the whole *raison d'être* of history and culture lies in the elaboration of a small number of exceptional personalities, original in quality and endowed with remarkable creative gifts; it would follow that the bulk of mankind was destined to be swallowed up in an impersonal and anonymous life. From the naturalist standpoint, this would be a very feasible solution, but it would not be a Christian one. Christianity affirms that every man has it in his power to become a personality, and that he must be afforded every opportunity of achieving this end. Every human personality has an intrinsic value, and cannot be reduced to a common denominator. All men are equal before God, and are called upon to share in the Eternal Life and the Kingdom of God. The deep-rooted inequality of men's gifts and qualities, vocations and merits, in no wise contradicts this assumption. In the case of the personality, this equality is founded upon a hierarchical order of original and diverse qualities. The ontological inequality between men is not determined by their social position, which is but a perversion of the true hierarchical order, but by their real qualities, gifts and merits. Thus the doctrine of the personality combines the aristocratic and democratic principles. A metaphysical system based on purely democratic principles is bound to misunderstand the problem of the personality; and such a misunderstanding is the result of a spiritual rather than a political error.

CHAPTER II

THE PERSONALITY AND THE GENERAL — THE PER-
SONALITY AND THE SPECIES—THE PERSONALITY AND
THE SUPRA-PERSONAL—MONISM AND PLURALISM—
THE ONE AND THE MULTIPLE

The problem of the personality is also related to the traditional problem of the general and the particular propounded by the Realist and Nominalist philosophies. It is commonly admitted that nominalism is more favourable to the personality than realism. The individualistic currents of European thought have always tended to be nominalist. The problem of the personality or of the individual plays no part in Greek philosophy. Platonism was apparently unable to conceive the possibility of a passage from non-Being to Being; it maintained that Being was individual only when added on to non-Being, and that it was general when non-Being was subtracted. But for the most part the problem of the 'general' has been misstated because its social and objective origin has usually been overlooked. The 'general' is not an existential, but a purely sociological category. The 'general', as opposed to the individual, is real only when it is itself individual and unique. The non-individual 'general' is a logical rather than an ontological category; and its logical significance is determined by the degree of community existing between conscious-nesses that have no bond of communion; in other words, since the terms objective and social are synonymous, its nature is fundamen-tally sociological. The concept of the 'general' is a product of social conditions which have nothing in common with communion. This concept serves to establish an identity, to make communication possible; but it does not make for 'familiarity' or inner communion. That is, indeed, the determining factor in the problem of the per-sonality. Objective and social processes give rise to number, which becomes the measure of all things in the sphere of the general. Society is governed by the law of number, whose sway also extends over knowledge in its social form. Where the law of number reigns supreme, where the part and the whole co-exist, there we are confronted with the object as an obstacle to authentic existence or the spiritual life. Spiritual life takes no account of number, its symbol is unity; it is not concerned with the categories of a divided world, the whole and the part, the general and the individual. Kierkegaard maintains that, from the religious standpoint, the individual has priority over the species. I am fully prepared to endorse this view on condition that the term 'personality' is substituted for that of the 'individual', which belongs to the same category as the notion of species. In defining the personality, it is important to conceive it as a whole and not as a part, as something that can never be a part. The personality is never anything *particular* as opposed to anything *general*. It can become a part either of society or of some other general whole only when it has been objectified. But intrinsically, the personality can never be a part of any *genus*, such as nature or society. The personality is spirit; and it belongs to the spiritual world which completely ignores any correlation of the part and the whole, of the individual and the general.

Solitude is the direct outcome of the pressure exerted on the personality by the natural and social worlds, of its conversion into object. But the personality has a creative function to perform in social and cosmic life. Spiritually, the personality is never isolated, for it postulates the existence of others, of the Thou and the We, without at the same time ever becoming a part or a means. The Ego's solitude is born of its objective existence; it occurs only in the natural world. That the category of number is inapplicable to the personality is best exemplified in the fact that one human personality may be worth more than two men, than a considerable number of men, or even a whole society of men. Ten men are not twice five men, nor a hundred men ten times ten men.

The personality is the principal category of existential knowledge. Both particularism and universalism are equally erroneous as the products of strictly rationalist thought obedient to the laws of an objective world. The antithesis of the universal and the particular is · a peculiarly objective one. The personality is not anything partial or particular. That is already manifest in the fact that it never constitutes a part of anything. The particular does not comprehend the

[131]

universal, and the error of particularism lies in its attempt to endow the particular with a universal character. That is, indeed, a grave temptation. The fact that the personality has a universal content is what distinguishes it from the particular and the partial. It can do what no *mere part* can aspire to do—it can realize itself in the process of making its content universal. It is a unity in the midst of plurality, and can thus comprehend the universe. From the standpoint of the objective world, however, the existence of the personality constitutes a paradox: *the personality is the incarnated antinomy of the individual and the social, of form and matter, of the infinite and the finite, of freedom and destiny.* For this reason, the personality cannot be a complete whole; it is not an objective *datum*; it fashions and creates itself, it is dynamic. It is essentially the union of the finite and the infinite. It would dissolve into nothing as soon as it discarded its limitations and supports, as soon as it merged in cosmic infinity. But the personality would not be the image and likeness of God, if it were not endowed with infinite capacity. No partial thing could comprehend this infinite content: the personality alone fulfils this rôle because it is indivisible. In that consists its essential mystery. The human personality alone represents the intersection point of several worlds, none of which completely contains it; in this way, it belongs only partially to any society, State, confession, or even the universe. The personality thus exists on several planes. The uni-plane existence advocated by monism can only undermine and destroy the basis of the personality; since the personality is all-comprehensive; it is not confined to any particular plane or system, although it always postulates a reality beyond that of its immediate awareness. A *logically* expounded nominalism is incapable of laying the foundations of a doctrine of the personality, because it tends to subdivide reality and to disintegrate the personality; it is quite incapable of grasping the personality as a whole.

Platonism is not a personalist philosophy but one of general principles. The Christian Revelation, in so far as it involved the idea of the personality and thereby could never adequately express itself through the medium of the Greek philosophical categories, contributed an absolutely new content. Nor is the doctrine of the personality expounded in the often more profound Hindoo philosophy, although monism is not its exclusive characteristic when we consider the diversity of the Hindoo philosophical system.[1] The *Atman* is the very foundation of the Ego, the kernel of the personality; the *Brahman* is the impersonal divinity. The doctrine of *Atman* may, indeed, be interpreted in the personalist sense. Throughout the history of philosophical thought, monism and pluralism have been constantly opposed, and have proved most difficult to reconcile. The fundamental problem is how to reconcile the doctrine of the unity of the Divine Personality with the plurality of human personalities. Christianity alone holds the key to this problem, and thus helps to enrich our philosophical knowledge. Dilthey very rightly maintains that metaphysical science is an historically limited fact, whereas the metaphysical consciousness of the personality is eternal.[2] No rationalist theory of metaphysics has known how to give expression to this consciousness. Existential philosophy alone is able to propound the problem of the personality.

There are various categories of the individuality in the objective, natural and social worlds. The 'nation' is one such category. Humanity is inconceivable in terms of an abstract, non qualitative unity; it is a concrete, qualitative unity comprehending all the categories of individuality. An exception must be made in the case of the State, which is only a simple function without any ontological value. But there is this difference between real values such as humanity, society, and nationality, which we encounter in the objective world, and the human personality, that the former are unable to experience any sense of joy and pain, while the latter is a living and concrete manifestation. From the standpoint of man's inner existence and destiny, these real values, although they appear to be supra-human, are the attributes of the qualities inherent in the human personality. The personality realizes itself concretely, through the qualitative values expressed in the relations of one or another group, of society, of the nation, of humanity. But as the image and likeness of God, it has a far greater ontological reality than the supra-personal realities dominating the objective world.

These propositions can be applied equally well to the problem of

[1] Cf. two new books on the history of Hindoo philosophy: O. Strauss, *Indische Philosophie*, and R. Grousset, *Les Philosophies Indiennes,* in two volumes. Cf. also: René Guénon, *L'Homme et son Devenir Selon le Vedanta.*

[2] Dilthey, *Einleitung in die Geisteswissenschaften.*

the relationship between the personality and the Idea. The *raison d'être* of the personality may lie in its allegiance to an idea for which it may, and sometimes must, sacrifice itself. But it must never be regarded merely as a means, as an instrument in the service of some idea. The idea should, on the contrary, be the means and instrument by which the personality can realize itself, grow, and achieve qualitative ascension. By its devotion to, and, if necessary, sacrifice and death for an idea, the personality will affirm its higher validity and, ultimately, acquire the symbolic expression of eternity. It concentrates in itself the whole mystery of Being, of Creation. The personality holds the supreme place in the scale of values. But its supreme value supposes an inherent content surpassing it, a suprapersonal element for which it is more than a mere instrument. God, Who is the source of all value, could never employ the personality as a means. If the contrary is true of society, of the nation, or of the State, their potentially dark and demoniac power is responsible. The personality alone can reveal the pure and original conscience, free from objectification, and sovereign in all matters. In the suprapersonal, social collectives, the conscience is objectified and its true nature is obscured. The existential conscience is forged in the struggle waged against social promptings and influences.

We have next to consider the personality in relation to the concept of universal order or harmony. Can the personality be regarded as a means of achieving universal order and harmony? That is the ancient, non-Christian conception of the personality adopted by Saint Augustine, which has since deformed the Christian consciousness. Saint Augustine believed that evil existed only in the parts, that the reintegration of these parts in universal order and harmony would mean the end of evil. In the light of this doctrine, Hell is good and just when representing the triumph of universal goodness, order and harmony. But in reality this doctrine denotes the triumph of the objective world over the mystery of the inner life, the supremacy of 'the general and the generic' over the individual and the personal. There could be nothing more anti-Christian or anti-human. The idea of universal order and harmony has no moral or spiritual value, because there is no implicit relationship with the personality's inner life. The concept of 'universal order' is derived entirely from the objective and degraded world; and there is some justification for the rebellion against it of Ivan Karamazov and of the hero of Dostoievsky's *Memoirs from Underground*. The dominance of general and generic principles, of social and universal concepts, in the spheres of speculation and ethics, invariably denotes a victory on the part of the degraded and objective world. The history of Christianity affords frequent examples of this tendency. Human existence acquires significance only when all human slavery is suppressed, or when the personality is freed from the dominance of the world, of the State, of the nation, or of abstract thought and ideas; when it is immediately subordinated to a living God. This free inner subordination to God, Who is never synonymous with the 'general', is the only condition which enables the human personality to determine from within its relations to the supra-personal values and general realities. In order that the personality may discover its true social nature and vocation, it is necessary that its existence and consciousness should be free from social pressure and the constraining influence of the general, the generic and the universal concepts. The spiritual personality does not belong to the generic category; it is not hereditary. There is even something distressing in family resemblance, which would appear to belie the unique and inimitable character of every personality. For this reason, a society aspiring to be a communion of personalities cannot be founded upon a typical form of objectification—the family; it can be founded only on spiritual fraternity. The completely realized personality is inimitable and self-sufficient. The Communist, Fascist and National-Socialist systems of education, based upon suggestion and imitation, are essentially anti-personalist. They tend to develop a sense of general order and harmony at the expense of the personality's self-realization. The terrifying idea of universal order threatens to reduce the personality to the level of a means; it is merely the objective formulation on a cosmic scale of a state of social necessity—itself one of the objective forms of the world's sinful degradation. Any objective idea is necessarily an obstacle to the development of the personality; it has validity only as an integral part of human existence. Man's further progress, his emancipation from the tyranny of the objective world, must depend upon the victory of spiritual and personal ties over generic relationships.

CHAPTER III

THE PERSONALITY AND SOCIETY—THE PERSONALITY AND THE MASS—THE PERSONALITY AND SOCIAL ARISTOCRATISM—SOCIAL PERSONALISM—THE PERSONALITY AND COMMUNION — COMMUNICATION AND COMMUNION

The problem of the personality in relation to society is not purely a problem of sociology or of social philosophy, but is essentially a problem of metaphysics and of Existential philosophy. As we have already shown, all the fundamental problems of knowledge can be envisaged from the standpoint either of society or of communion. Knowledge can be either social, concerned primarily with the material world, or it can be concerned above all with communion, with the revelation of the mystery of existence. Intuition is the foundation of communion, the faculty of being able to identify oneself with all things. Communion alleviates the nostalgia associated with solitude. The personality and the spiritual community stand in a different relationship to each other in society and in communion. In the case of communion, the community becomes a part of the personality and endows it with a special quality. In the case of society, on the other hand, the personality is merely a part of the community. The social aspect of communion is primarily the concern of the personality thus rescued from solitude. The personality's self-realization supposes communion. Its content and vocation are by nature social, but are not determined by society; their social determination comes from within. Thus the personality affirms its supreme value even in the sphere of social life.

The personality and society are not identical, as the various social doctrines upholding the organic theory of society would maintain. The function of society is to establish a more or less permanent and stable mode of communication between men; it is a material phenomenon manifesting itself in the degraded world; its rule is the law of the greatest number. In other words, society is a means of organizing the life of the masses. Society fails to be communion because it can offer no solution of the problem of solitude. In the material world, in the world of objects, true communion and community are supplanted by a socially organized collective. Thus, the relations of the personality to society can be interpreted both from within and from without: from the standpoint of naturalism and sociology, and from that of spiritual and Existential philosophy. In the light of positivist sociology, the personality is merely a part, a minute part of society. Society is an infinitely more powerful thing than the personality. The relationship between them is based upon quantitative categories, which afford no real solution of the problem of value. But when regarded from within, from the existential and spiritual standpoint, society is a part of the presonality; it becomes a qualitative content acquired by the personality in the process of self-realization. Thus the personality comprehends society, although it is not wholly identifiable with it. As Vinet has very justly pointed out, society is not the entire man, but only an association of men.[1] There is a region in the depths of the personality which remains absolutely impenetrable to society; the personality's spiritual life eludes society and cannot be determined by it. The spiritual life is the path leading to communion, to the Kingdom of God. But some of the aspects of this spiritual life may be expressed in social forms; thus religion tends to become a social phenomenon and the Kingdom of God a social institution. Here we touch upon the two sources of religion discussed by Bergson.[2] The personality, indeed, can never be a part of society, because it can never be a part of anything, because it can only participate in communion.

Needless to say, the State represents an extreme form of materialization. The State fails to take into account the mystery of the personality, even when it claims to uphold its rights; for it regards the personality as an abstract unity rather than as a living entity. The State is not existential; it contains no existential element such as that inherent in the notion of 'country', no warmth or life. Its function is merely objective; it is, in fact, the very antithesis of communion.

[1] Cf. Vinet, *Essais sur la manifestation des Convictions religieuses et sur la séparation de l'Eglise et de l'Etat.*

[2] *Vide* Bergson's *The Two Sources of Morality and Religion.*

Communion is never the proper function of the State; its presence is invariably the sign of another category of values. Toennies established a distinction between organic communities (*Gemeinschaft*), such as the family, the tribe, the people, on the one hand, and ideological, mechanical or social formations (*Gesellschaft*), such as the State, on the other. He failed, however, to see the problem of communion in its true light, because he was content to consider organic communities from a naturalist standpoint. The organic conception of society favoured by the romantics is a form of naturalism. Communion, on the other hand, is a spiritual phenomenon transcending organic nature. Thus Guardini opposes Gemeinschaft (*communion*) to *Organization*.[1] The organic and the naturalist conceptions of the people or of the social collective tend to regard the personality as a simple cell of the national organization, as merely a part of the whole.[2] This tendency may be observed in all the popularist ideologies such as Fascism, Hitlerism, and Eurasianism. The power of a society, and particularly of a State, does not constitute a criterion; such power may, indeed, prove to be a demoniac manifestation. The personality's highest value may lie precisely in its weakness when confronted with either society or the State; for it would be a mistake to attach a maximum value to the rule of force in a degraded and material world. Man himself should be assessed higher than either society, the nation or the State, even though these latter may have the power to oppress and enslave him in a world where all relationships are based upon compulsion. The function of the objective social world is to introduce order, law and authority. That is the essence of any sociological conception. The world may also be conceived exclusively in terms of labour, in terms of an analogy between the world or social life and a workshop or a factory. But the fact is generally overlooked that a philosophy of labour must be anti-materialist, that labour is an essentially spiritual and psychic rather than a purely material thing as Marx interpreted it.[3] By that

[1] *Vide* Romano Guardini's *Vom Sinn der Kirche.*

[2] In his *Struggle for the Personality*, N. Mikhailovsky, a Russian sociologist of the 1870's, shows a great comprehension of the problem. But philosophically he is quite incompetent. He fails to grasp that the struggle for the personality ought to be pursued spiritually rather than biologically.

[3] Cf. A. Bogdanov, the marxist empiriomonist, in his *Tectologie* and *Science Générale de l'Organisation.*

I mean, that labour can be a basis of communion as well as of society,[1] in so far as it represents a quality of the personality. In Communism there is merely communication which is forcibly made to assume a character of communion. The exploitation of man by man, as well as the exploitation of man by the State, is a way of converting man into an object. The only way to abolish the exploitation of man by man is to confront the Ego with the Thou. Neither capitalism nor materialist Communism is capable of this.[2]

There is a fundamental difference between communication and communion. The communication between consciousnesses invariably supposes a state of disintegration and dissociation. It embraces a variety of degrees ranging from the strong and intimate family bonds to the looser and more remote ties binding the individual to the State. But communication can never become communion, human fraternity or love. Socialism may be able to free the personality from narrower forms of association and their implicit forms of communication. But communion can never result from the Ego's association with the object. In its social life, the Ego is constantly confronted with objects, and any communication between them must suppose a state of disintegration. But communion does away with the objective world. The family is an objective form of the *erotic* and affective life, and, for this reason, it often encourages communication at the expense of communion. The State is a tyrant when it attempts to enforce communion—its very antithesis. Compulsion is the necessary condition of a world governed by means of communication. The material world is a disintegrated world whose parts are isolated from each other despite their external cohesion. Communion, as we have already explained, can only take place between the Ego and the Thou, between one Ego and another; and never between the Ego and the object, society or the *Es*. The communion of the Ego and the Thou gives rise to the We; the communion of two personalities is consummated in a third. The same is true of the Ego's communication with the object; in this case, however, the third person is the *Es*. Nature and the natural laws,

[1] Cf. Haessle, *Le Travail*. The work was written from the Thomist point of view.

[2] Cf. an interesting book, *La Revolution Nécessaire*, by Aron and Dandieu. It approaches social problems from the personalist standpoint. It sums up the investigations of young Frenchmen of to-day in this domain.

[139]

society, the State, the family, the class, are all so many *Es* or It, when confronted with the personality. Cognitive and emotional communion can only be realized in the existential sphere, in relation to an existing being; it invariably denotes an awareness of another world. The objective social world is a quantitative world. The *One* and the *It* are symbols of a degraded world abstracted from communion, from intuition and love, in other words, of a world of mere external communication. This world can have no conception of spiritual union. In it the Church and the religious community also become a means of social and objective communication; for the Church can be envisaged as a society as well as a communion. From the social standpoint, the Church represents a secondary and reflected world of symbolic communication. Objective and social communications are symbolic rather than real. The distinguishing characteristic of communion is its ontological reality; the symbolism of communication excludes all but conventional signs. Each social group, be it the family, the class, the State, the Church (as a social institution), has its own peculiar symbolism. In such groups the inner life or the affective life may be more or less manifest, but authentic communion always remains inaccessible. Both union and communion suppose a maximum degree of spiritual community. But a monastery or a religious community fails to be a true community, since it is founded only on the symbolism of communication; monastic life is invariably a form of social objectification.

We should have some hesitation in accepting Leibnitz's theory of the completely finite monad. Jaspers very rightly postulates that one Ego is accessible to another, to the Thou.[1] As a corollary, the Ego also postulates the We, in whose depths the communion of the Ego and the Thou is achieved. But the monad may be more or less hermetic; it may be closed to some objects and open to others. We must understand this dynamically. Thus the monad may have its doors and windows shut to the spiritual side of life, and will consequently experience extreme solitude. But it does so by virtue of its peculiar destiny rather than by virtue of its metaphysical definition. Creative personalities and geniuses especially may experience great difficulties in their relations with the commonplace everyday

[1] Cf. Jaspers, in the second volume of his *Existenzerhellung*, the most interesting part of his philosophy.

world; they may be antagonistic to this world while at the same time apprehending the universe through it. The symbolism of social communications is variable. In this connection, both technology and the machine are of the utmost importance. Technology helps to improve communication between men, but far from diminishing their fundamental disunion, it only tends to increase it. Technology represents an extreme form of the materialization of human existence and, as such, it is not concerned with communion. The motor car, the aeroplane, the cinema, the wireless, all these inventions have certainly contributed a great deal to make communication between men universal; thanks to them, man has been able to liberate himself from the determination of a particular locality and to give himself up to the current of universal life. But the prodigious diffusion of these universal means of communication tends to undermine the intimacy and familiarity so essential to communion; it has the effect of making man extremely solitary. This process, like everything else in the world, has two aspects: a positive and a negative one. In the restricted societies of the past, patriarchal or generic, individuals communicated with each other in a too impersonal manner. In order to make these relations more personal it was necessary that man should experience solitude and that the Ego should become detached from its all-absorbing organic ties. Technology has greatly contributed to this end. The use of machinery has to a large extent done away with the exploitation of man and animal, which was an obstacle to communion. In this technological age we have to admit the possibility of communion with animals as a means of overcoming our solitude. When confronted with the Ego, the dog may prove to be a true friend rather than an object. In this sense new perspectives are opening to us. The change brought about in the relations between men, between man and God, between man and animal or flower, is invariably the sign of a higher purpose than that manifest in the organization of industrial concerns.

The significance of communion as a goal of human life is essentially religious. Communion involves participation, reciprocal participation, interpenetration. This participation must take place in the very heart of the Ego's union with the Thou. The interpenetration of the Ego and the Thou is consummated in God. Communion resolves the antitheses of the one and the multiple, of the

[141]

particular and the universal. In the eyes of society, the personality is always irrational by virtue of its inner life, of its unique destiny. To rationalize this destiny society has to resort to compulsion. Personalities may also unite to form secret societies, like Freemasonry or other occult societies; but these secret societies do not pave the way to communion because their character is essentially 'social'.[1] Indeed, the personality may find itself in greater bondage than ever. No degree of communication within a given social group can put an end to the antagonism between the personality and its social environment. This fundamental conflict is the eternal tragedy of human life. Class antagonisms and conflicts can be resolved; but that is not the case of the antagonism and conflict engendered by the confrontation of the personality and of society. Marx only saw in this conflict a disguised form of class war. He concluded that the advent of a classless society would resolve all such conflict, by making the personality completely 'social' and satisfied. But Marx failed to take into account the deeper aspects of the problem. The very contrary is true. A class war is only a mask of the eternal and metaphysical conflict of the personality and society. In former times, the oppressed personality of one or another class, whether bourgeois, proletarian or intellectual, would rise up in revolt against the omnipotent and absolute State. Thus the State or society was always prevented from becoming definitely absolute. In his *Fascism*, Mussolini argues that the necessity of respecting the rights of the oppressed personality of one or another social class will disappear when the People shall finally become master of the State and the State shall become absolute. Thus both Communism and Fascism have the same reason for eliminating the conflict between the personality and society; in fact, from the standpoint of social morphology, these systems constitute a similar type. Fascism certainly represents a new and logical form of democracy in which the people claims to be the direct master of the State and makes of the State an absolute expression of its essence. In reality, Fascism is more opposed to an aristocratic and liberal system of government than to a democratic one, which, if logically developed, must culminate in State control. Was Roman Caesarism not democratic? Indeed, Caesarism has always been markedly plebeian in character. Mankind will probably

[1] Cf. Simmel, *Soziologie*.

have to pass through a stage of purely social unification in which all class distinctions will be abolished. A unified and henceforth classless people will be master of the State, and the human personality, definitely become a social object, will experience no antagonism to society. But then, at the height of this purely social process, when class antagonisms shall have ceased to mask the essential features of human existence, we shall behold the re-emergence of the eternal and tragic conflict between the human personality and the State. But at that stage, the personality will not be identified with one or another group; it will represent a complete whole, envisaged as the image and likeness of God. The world will again behold the human personality in revolt against the people, against society, against the State. Marx made many valuable sociological discoveries, but, for the most part, they were confined to the secondary sphere of existence. Proudhon had a far deeper vision of the eternal antinomy of the personality and of society. Neither marxism nor any other materialist socialist system attempts to deal with the problems of solitude and of communion as distinct from the problem of communication, because these systems fail to apprehend the profound metaphysical significance of the problem of the personality.[1] The problem we must now consider is that of the personality in relation to the mass or the social collective, to aristocracy and democracy.

Have we any foundation for saying that the union of personalities in a social collective represents the attainment of the We? Is the authentic union or communion of the Ego and Thou attainable under these conditions? Certainly not. There can be no doubt that the social collective is part of the objective sphere of human existence. The life of the masses is governed by the anti-personal law of collective suggestion.[2] When it is surrendered to the impulse, the collective suggestion, the imitative instinct and the baser emotions of the mass, the life of the personality becomes qualitatively impoverished. The mass instinct is not that of an organized people. Nor is the mass the expression of the We. If the human Ego fails to experience solitude when plunged into the elementary, unconscious and exclusively emotional state of the mass, that is not because it

[1] Cf. *Die Sozialistische Entscheidung,* a new book by Tillich, the leader of German religious socialism. Tillich does not propound the existential problem of the personality. [2] *Vide* on this subject, *Le Bon, Freud, Simmel.*

[143]

has attained to communion with the Thou or union with another Being, but simply because its peculiar feeling and consciousness have been swallowed up in the *Es* or It. Thus the mass or crowd represents the *Es* or It, for the We supposes the existence of another Ego or Thou. When confronted with the mass, the Ego is forced to impersonate a character imposed upon it by the mass, and to adopt its unconscious instincts and passions. Simmel even ventures to say that this impersonation or mask is the manifestation of mass power. The imitative instinct is the determining factor in the life of the masses.[1] The Ego overcomes its solitude at the expense of the Self. Thus in time of war and revolution, or during periods of reaction, in the blind fury of collective, national or religious movements, we can observe the social collective in action. In such a state there is neither solitude nor communion. Thus Russian Communism claims to have abolished the sense of human solitude; but it has, at the same time, made communion impossible between the Ego and the Thou. This is equally, and even perhaps to a greater degree, true of the German National Socialist ideal of collective society, which is certainly founded on the *Es* rather than on the oecumenical We. In National Socialism we behold the rationalization of impersonal instincts and inclinations. Mass-leaders are like mediums; they sway the masses, but are also swayed by them. Freud very justly notes that the leader exercises an erotic fascination on the mass, that they are infatuated by him.[2] It is this fact which makes possible the dictatorship of a Caesar, a Cromwell, a Napoleon, or of the little Caesars and Napoleons of to-day. The same erotic atmosphere usually surrounds the monarch, although the powers of the monarchy were based on more stable, traditional and religiously sanctioned emotions. The leader must discover a symbolism capable not only of exciting but also of uniting the masses, and of binding them to him. This symbolism, however, must always flatter the mass psychology. The leader cannot do otherwise than flatter the mass. And if he happens to be an exceptional man, he may experience a poignant sense of solitude, a sense of thwarted communion, while surrendering his personality entirely to the mass. The more ordinary type of monarch is equally far removed from communion and from the understand-

[1] Cf. Tarde, *De L'Imitation.*

[2] Freud, *Essais de Psycho-analyse* and *Psychologie Collective et Analyse du Moi.*

ing of the symbolism of his position in relation to his subjects. The man of genius, the great historical personality, the mass leader, is the most solitary of men; for the ties that bind the leader to the masses are those that govern the relationship of the subject to the object, rather than of the Ego to the Thou. But how is the personality related to the peace-loving democracies which assure the masses a comparatively stable government? Their relationship demonstrates the tragic, eternal and ineluctable conflict between the personality and society. Public opinion in democratic countries represents an extreme form of social materialization, since it is educated to a general level of mediocrity at the expense of the personality's inner life. Bourgeois individualism, with its essentially hermetic and stifling vetos and prohibitions, allies itself easily with a complete impersonalism, with a levelling down of all values, and with the basest forms of social imitation. The realization of the personality is an essentially aristocratic task, although it has nothing in common with established social and political aristocracies. This latter is a generic and an hereditary form of aristocracy, sanctified by tradition, although it may no longer have anything in common with personal qualities.[1] But we are concerned above all with personal aristocracy, with the expression of man's inner life. It is, above all, a question of man's personal dignity, of a *real* rather than of a symbolic dignity, inseparable from the personality's qualities and gifts. The generic social dignity is symbolic, being the heritage of the past and the property of a nation, a class, a caste. Democracy, in so far as it affirms the dignity of every man, expresses a deeper truth. It errs, however, in emphasizing the material aspects of human existence. No society is capable of appeasing the nostalgia for communion, for familiarity, for union with a kindred soul, for the true reflection of one Ego in another. Every society is Caesar's, whereas true communion is the Kingdom of God. The nostalgia inherent in solitude is the soul's nostalgia. To escape from solitude is to embrace the spiritual life. The path of communion is beset with difficulties and pain because each personality represents a distinct and mysterious world only partially accessible to another personality. But when the personality enters into the spiritual world, it is permeated with an atmosphere of unity and fraternity, which is the Kingdom of God.

[1] Cf. Berdyaev, *Christianity and Class War.*

CHAPTER IV

THE PERSONALITY AND CHANGE—THE PERSONALITY
AND LOVE — THE PERSONALITY AND DEATH — THE
OLD AND THE NEW MAN—CONCLUSIONS

As we have already noted, the essence of the personality is immutable. The personality suffers change in the process of self-
realization, but its identity is not thereby altered. There is every
reason to rejoice in a change that enriches and exalts the personality,
just as there is every reason to deplore a change that deforms it or
alters it beyond recognition. The personality is eternal, identical and
unique; but for all that, it is permanently in a process of creative
change because it has need of time to realize its potentialities to the
full. It must always endeavour to resolve contradictions.[1] Although
it is fundamentally hostile to time, the synonym of death, it engenders time in the process of self-development. Thus its paradoxical
nature can reconcile change and immutability, time and the supra-
temporal. The personality is anything but static; its very nature
postulates change and creative innovation; but it endeavours to
reconcile change with the preservation of its fundamental identity
and character. It exists by virtue of a mysterious alliance between
change and innovation, on the one hand, and constancy and self-
preservation, on the other. In defining the human personality, stress
should be laid on its fundamental consistency and on the persistence
of its identity despite many outward changes and the acquisition of
many new characteristics. This alliance is best exemplified in man's
consciousness of a vocation and a predestination in which, indeed,
change and creation are reconciled with the preservation of the
personal identity as the integral constituents of a unified life directed
towards a higher goal. As a rule, men fail to account for the survival
of personal identity in the face of apparent changes. But the mystery
of the personality, that of its unique content, is best revealed in love

[1] Cf. Le Sonne's very interesting book, *Le Devoir*.

and is, for that reason, veiled from those who are not lovers. The identity of another's personality must often remain obscure when love, sympathy or goodwill are withheld. The life of the personality is most intimately associated with love, without which there is no self-fulfilment, no overcoming of isolation, no communion. Love in its turn postulates the personality: it is the relationship of one personality to another, the means of freeing the personality from the prison of self and of allowing it to identify itself with another personality—the act by which it receives eternal acknowledgment and confirmation.[1] The conception of love is absent from monism, which affirms not the identity of the personality, but that of all personalities—the inherence of one and the same principle in all, the identity of the Ego and the Thou. The essential quality of love, on the other hand, consists in the discovery of another's unique personality, in the fact that the personality expands only in relation to another personality. Love is therefore dualistic because it supposes two personalities in place of an undifferentiated identity. The fact that each personality is unique, that it constitutes a Thou, is essential to our understanding of the mystery of love. Without it the personality would be incomprehensible. Personalism affirms the love of a concrete and living being, of a Thou, as opposed to the love of 'goodness' or of an abstract idea. The love of 'goodness' can easily degenerate into the love of the It (*Es*). Personalism stands for the love of one's fellow-beings, of the unique personality, of Divine humanity, as distinct from the love of God and of man's supra-personal value. At this point, we have a confrontation of idealist and realist ethics: the former affirm the love of the Idea and of Value; the latter, the love of man *per se*. But surely the love of man *per se* should not exclude the love of value, of quality and of degree. On the contrary, all these should co-exist, just as the human and the supra-human, the real and the ideal, co-exist in the personality itself. To be in love with another's personality is to perceive the identity and unity underlying its perpetual change and division; it is to perceive its nobility even in the midst of utter degradation. Love is the means by which the obscurity of the objective world is illuminated and the heart of existence is penetrated, so that the Thou may displace and, finally, annihilate

[1] Cf. Max Scheller, *Nature et Formes de la Sympathie.*

the object. Thus authentic love is invariably the herald of the coming of the Kingdom of God, of another plane of Being, distinct from the degraded objective world wherein human life is not only perpetual change but also constant betrayal. In this degraded world man's identity is eclipsed, his personality is disintegrated, and its unique image is shrouded in obscurity. In such a world there can be no communion, since the personality and all its attributes are spurned and despised. But the cause of the personality still has a champion in the powerful forces of memory, love and the creative instincts. For the purposes of social life, of society, it is not essential to preserve the identity of the personality, but there can be no communion without it.

We cannot dispense with love in our relations with others or with ourselves. The egoist is not necessarily a man who loves himself. He may, indeed, detest himself and, for that very reason, bear a grudge against other people. This sense of humiliation may induce him to seek compensation in cruelty to others.[1] The egoist may therefore be at war with himself as well as with other people. We are told, 'Love thy neighbour as thyself!' This does imply that we should love ourselves, that we should identify ourselves lovingly with our own personality, with its unique essence. Extreme self-hate can only obscure our awareness of the personality, since this awareness is founded upon love as the intuition of the personality. We should endeavour to exercise this intuition about our own selves as well as about others, for we cannot be expected to starve ourselves of love even when bidden to make a sacrifice of ourselves. Thus the development of the personality implies sacrifice and renunciation, the ultimate triumph over egocentrism, but never self-hate.

Pain and suffering are the necessary accompaniment of the personality's attempt at self-fulfilment. Men have often preferred to renounce the attempt rather than face the pain. Thus the Communist repudiation of the personality is the outcome of the desire to banish pain and suffering; and communism hopes to achieve this end through the collective organization not only of social life, but also of the human consciousness. The struggle to realize the personality is an heroic one. Heroism is above all a personal act. The

[1] The fundamental idea underlying Adler's theory.

[148]

personality is not only related to freedom, but cannot exist without it. To realize the personality is therefore to achieve inner freedom, to liberate man from all external determination. There can be consciousness of freedom in a state of being governed by necessity. But the consciousness of freedom is a heavy burden for man to bear; pain and suffering are its accompaniment, and tragedy the outcome.[1] To avoid these consequences, to escape the tragic solution, men often deliberately sacrifice their freedom. Thus two rival theories of existence are to be found constantly opposed: the one assigns as man's goal an altogether negative salvation, a freedom synonymous with damnation, a freedom from all suffering in time and eternity; the other maintains that the *summum bonum* lies in man's self-realization, in the personality's development and qualitative ascension, in the attainment of truth and beauty, in short, in the creative life. Man's quest for salvation may prove to be only the supernatural projection of his terrestrial egoism. But needless to say, this quest may also be interpreted as the means of attaining the complete and perfect life. To achieve this life, man must be armed with unwavering courage, he must affirm the validity of his personality as against the anxious fear of life and death, as against the fears engendered by utilitarian considerations and the anxiety to be happy regardless of any preoccupation with freedom and perfection. The personalist principle is the very antithesis of the individual or social utilitarian principle: it affirms that, from the social standpoint, every personality must be situated in a condition of human existence corresponding to its human dignity.

The personality's tragic existence in this world is essentially the outcome of its close kinship with death, whose mystery does not affect the impersonal. By virtue of its essence or 'idea', the personality is both immortal and eternal; but our world is especially fatal to everything immortal and eternal. For that reason, the personality is most in danger of death when nearest to self-realization. Its purpose and idea are an inherent part of the eternal order of the universe. Therefore, there is nothing so tragic as the death of a man about to realize his personality. But even if we were to admit the possibility of attaining to natural immortality through the complete repudiation of the personality, this sort of immortality has nothing in

[1] Cf. Berdyaev's *Dostoievsky* and *Freedom and the Spirit*.

common with eternity. The cause of the personality is that of man's liberation from his natural state of servitude. Man was, first of all, a slave of nature; then he became a slave, in turn, of the State, of the nation, of a class, and, finally, of technology and of organized society. But man's self-realization is accompanied by his emancipation from all servitude, by his domination of all things. There is, however, a servitude from which no Utopia or social organization can liberate him—and that is the ultimate power of death. To triumph over death is to acknowledge its mystery; it is to adopt an antinomian attitude. It is also true that self-realization paves the way to communion in both the social and the cosmic spheres of life, and thus helps to transcend that state of isolation which is akin to death. To achieve communion is to have no fear of death; it is to feel that the power of love is stronger than that of death. Those who have achieved communion are not spared the tragic divorce of death, but for them this divorce is only confined to the natural world. Inwardly, in the spiritual world, it proves the path of true life, since death affects only the objective world and, especially, the personality of those who have surrendered themselves to its alien power. Self-realization is a process of permanent auto-creation, an elaboration of the new man at the expense of the old. When we speak of the emergence of the 'new man', we do not imply subservience to the temporal or the repudiation of man's eternal content, but we invoke rather the fulfilment of that eternal content. Change, innovation and creation are no doubt implied in the process of realizing the divine image and likeness in man, but in a quite different sense from that of the actualist conception of the new man in a technological age. The actualist theory of man dispenses with the idea of eternity. It does no more than confront the Ego with the object, to precipitate the Ego into an objective world. The Ego must, indeed, fulfil itself in the objective world as well, if all the aspects of the personality (including knowledge) are to be completely developed; but its objective development can never, and in no sense, be definitive. The complete realization of the personality can only take place on an extra-natural plane—on a plane of spiritual freedom, of communion and of love.

Man is an historical being; he seeks to realize himself in history, and his destiny is, therefore, historical. His life and his creative acts are restricted to the framework of history. Within this framework he is forced to give an objective form to his creative imagination. Indeed, man's failure to realize his dreams can be attributed directly to the fact that his creative acts are historically formulated. By virtue of its objective nature, history is absolutely indifferent to the human personality, for which it would appear to have even less regard than for nature; it has steadily refused to acknowledge the supreme value of the personality, for, if it did so, it would have no more *raison d'être*. And yet, for fear of impoverishing and diminishing himself, man cannot refuse to participate in history—his appointed path, his destiny. But he must take care never to become merely historically minded, never to found his criteria merely upon historical necessity. The task of creating culture devolves on man by virtue of his historical existence. Culture is also his path and destiny; and in the elaboration of cultural values he helps to fulfil himself as a creative being. Culture rescues man from a state of primitive barbarism and elevates him; but it also gives an objective form to his creative acts. Classical culture is the perfect form of man's objectified activity in the spheres of religion, morality, science, art and law. The ultimate effect of objective form is to extinguish man's creative fire and to weaken his creative urge, subjecting them both to the rule of law. It becomes a sort of stasis impeding the possibility of any transfiguration in the world. The supreme values of an established culture are as indifferent to man's inner life, as cruelly disposed towards the human personality, as the historical and natural worlds. This being so, culture has also its Day of Judgment—it will be judged by those who have helped to create it. Cultural idolatry is as reprehensible as barbarism. But there is no alternative: we have to face this tragic conflict, this insoluble antinomy, and assume full responsibility for it. There is no alternative but to shoulder the burden of history and culture, the burden of the terrifying, distressing and degraded world. Our only escape lies in the knowledge that there is an ultimate solution in the extra-natural sphere of Being, in which we participate also by virtue of our spiritual life. There, on the threshold of eternity, our consciousness fortified by tragic experience transcends the objective world.

Man is the dominating idea of my life—man's image, his creative freedom and his creative predestination. That is, too, the theme of the book which is now approaching its conclusion. But to treat of man is also to treat of God. And that, for me, is the essential point. The problem of man's 'centrality', of his creative activity, has never been seriously investigated by either Patristic thought or Scholastic philosophy. Renaissance humanism made the first important discoveries in this direction.[1] But the time has now come to pose this problem in a different way, for Renaissance humanism was still largely naturalistic in its outlook. In our time speculative thought tends to be more pessimistic, but at the same time it is more sensitive to the evils and sufferings of the world. Its pessimism is not passive; it attempts to grapple with the evils of the world. It is an active and creative pessimism. That is, again, one of my fundamental themes. In the present book I have attempted to expound this theme in the form of an essay on Existential philosophy. Feuerbach had made some headway in this direction when he tried to bridge the gulf between God and man. After him, Nietzsche advanced a step further when he propounded his idea of the superman. At this point man became merely an instrument or a means of transition, and he was, moreover, destined to become conscious of himself as such. At the present time, it is imperative to understand once more that the rediscovery of man will also be the rediscovery of God. That is the essential theme of Christianity. The philosophy of human existence is a Christian, a theandric philosophy. Truth is its supreme criterion. But truth is not an objective state, nor can it be apprehended like an object. Truth implies above all man's spiritual activity. Its apprehension depends on the degree of community between men, on their communion in the spirit.

[1] The most remarkable ideas of that age, and the ones nearest to my way of thinking, are those evolved by Pico della Mirandola and Paracelsus.

A BRIEF OVERVIEW OF
NIKOLAI BERDYAEV'S LIFE AND WORKS

Nikolai Berdyaev (1874–1948) was one of the greatest religious thinkers of the 20th century. His adult life, led in
Russia and in western European exile, spanned such cataclys-
mic events as the Great War, the rise of Bolshevism and the
Russian Revolution, the upsurge of Nazism, and the Second
World War. He produced profound commentaries on many of
these events, and had many acute things to say about the role
of Russia in the evolution of world history. There was sometimes almost no separation between him and these events: for
example, he wrote the book on Dostoevsky while revolutionary gunfire was rattling outside his window.

Berdyaev's thought is primarily a religious metaphysics,
influenced not only by philosophers like Kant, Hegel, Schopenhauer, Solovyov, and Nietzsche, but also by religious thinkers
and mystics such as Meister Eckhart, Angelus Silesius, Franz
van Baader, Jakob Boehme, and Dostoevsky. The most fundamental concept of this metaphysics is that of the *Ungrund* (a
term taken from Boehme), which is the pure potentiality of
being, the negative ground essential for the realization of the
novel, creative aspects of existence. A crucial element of Berdyaev's thought is his philosophical anthropology: A human
being is originally an "ego" out which a "person" must develop.
Only when an ego freely acts to realize its own concrete
essence, rather than abstract or arbitrary goals, does it become
a person. A society that furthers the goal of the development of
egos into persons is a true community, and the relation then
existing among its members is a sobornost.

He showed an interest in philosophy early on, at the age of
fourteen reading the works of Kant, Hegel, and Schopenhauer.

While a student at St. Vladimir's University in Kiev, he began to participate in the revolutionary Social-Democratic movement and to study Marxism. In 1898, he was sentenced to one month in a Kiev prison for his participation in an anti-government student demonstration, and was later exiled for two years (1901–02) to Vologda, in the north of Russia.

His first book, *Subjectivism and Individualism in Social Philosophy* (1901), represented the climax of his infatuation with Marxism as a methodology of social analysis, which he attempted to combine with a neo-Kantian ethics. However, as early as 1903, he took the path from "Marxism to idealism," which had already been followed by such former Marxists as Peter Struve, Sergey Bulgakov, and S. L. Frank. In 1904 Berdyaev became a contributor to the philosophical magazine *New Path*. The same year he married Lydia Trushcheva, a daughter of a Petersburg lawyer. In 1905–06, together with Sergey Bulgakov, he edited the magazine *Questions of Life*, attempting to make it the central organ of new tendencies in the domains of socio-political philosophy, religious philosophy, and art. The influence exerted upon him by the writers and philosophers Dmitry Merezhkovsy and Zinaida Gippius, during meetings with them in Paris in the winter of 1907–08, led him to embrace the Russian Orthodox faith. After his return to Russia, he joined the circle of Moscow Orthodox philosophers united around the Path publishing house (notably Bulgakov and Pavel Florensky) and took an active part in organizing the religious-philosophical Association in Memory of V. Solovyov. An important event in his life at this time was the publication of his article "Philosophical Truth and the Truth of the Intelligentsia" in the famous and controversial collection *Landmarks* (1909), which subjected to a critical examination the foundations of the world-outlook of the left-wing Russian intelligentsia. Around this time, Berdyaev published a work which inaugurated his life-long exploration of the concept of freedom in its many varieties and ramifications. In *The Philosophy of Freedom* (1911), a critique of the "pan-gnoseologism" of recent German and Russian philosophy led Berdyaev to a search for an authentically Christian ontology. The end result of this search was a philosophy of freedom, according to which human beings are rooted in a sobornost of being and thus possess true knowledge.

In 1916, Berdyaev published the most important work of his early period: *The Meaning of the Creative Act*. The originality of this work is rooted in the rejection of theodicy as a traditional problem of the Christian consciousness, as well as in a refusal to accept the view that creation and revelation have come to an end and are complete. The central element of the "meaning of the creative act" is the idea that man reveals his true essence in the course of a continuing creation realized jointly with God (a theurgy). Berdyaev's notion of "theurgy" (in contrast to those of Solovyov and Nikolai Fyodorov) is distinguished by the inclusion of the element of freedom: the creative act is a means for the positive self-definition of freedom not as the choice and self-definition of persons in the world but as a "foundationless foundation of being" over which God the creator has no power.

Berdyaev's work from 1914 to 1924 can be viewed as being largely influenced by his inner experience of the Great War and the Russian Revolution. His main themes during this period are the "cosmic collapse of humanity" and the effort to preserve the hierarchical order of being (what he called "hierarchical personalism"). Revolutionary violence and nihilism were seen to be directly opposed to the creatively spiritual transformation of "this world" into a divine "cosmos." In opposing the chaotic nihilism of the first year of the Revolution, Berdyaev looked for support in the holy ontology of the world, i.e., in the divine cosmic order. The principle of hierarchical inequality, which is rooted in this ontology, allowed him to nullify the main argument of the leveling ideology and praxis of Communism—the demand for "social justice." Berdyaev expressed this view in his *Philosophy of Inequality* (1923).

During this period, Berdyaev posed the theme of Russian

messianism in all its acuteness. Torn apart by the extremes of apocalyptic yearning and nihilism, Russia is placed into the world as the "node of universal history" (the "East-West"), in which are focused all the world's problems and the possibility of their resolution, in the eschatological sense. In the fall of the monarchy in February 1917, Berdyaev saw an opportunity to throw off the provincial Russian empire which had nothing in common with Russia's messianic mission. But the Russian people betrayed the "Russian idea" by embracing the falsehood of Bolshevism in the October Revolution. The Russian messianic idea nevertheless remains true in its ontological core despite this betrayal.

In the fall of 1919, Berdyaev organized in Moscow the Free Academy of Spiritual Culture, where he led a seminar on Dostoevsky and conducted courses on the Philosophy of Religion and the Philosophy of History. This latter course became the basis of one of his most important works: *The Meaning of History: An Essay on the Philosophy of Human Destiny* (1923). His attacks against the Bolshevik regime became increasingly intense: he called the Bolsheviks nihilists and annihilators of all spiritual values and culture in Russia. His activities and statements, which made him a notable figure in post-revolutionary Moscow, began to attract the attention of the Soviet authorities. In 1920, he was arrested in connection with the so-called "tactical center" affair, but was freed without any consequences. In 1922, he was arrested again, but this time he was expelled from Russia on the so-called "philosopher's ship" with other ideological opponents of the regime such as Bulgakov, Frank, and Struve.

Having ended up in Berlin, Berdyaev gradually entered the sphere of post-War European philosophy; he met Spengler, von Keyserling, and Scheler. His book *The New Middle Ages: Reflections on the Destiny of Russia and Europe* (1924) (English title: *The End of Our Time*) brought him European celebrity. Asserting that modern history has come to an end, and that it has been a failure, Berdyaev again claimed that Russia (now the post-revolutionary one) had a messianic mission. He wrote that "culture is now not just European; it is becoming universal. Russia, which had stood at the center of East and West, is now—even if by a terrible and catastrophic path—acquiring an increasingly palpable world significance, coming to occupy the center of the world's attention" (*The New Middle Ages*, p. 36). In 1924, Berdyaev moved to Paris, where he became a founder and professor of the Russian Religious-Philosophical Academy. In 1925, he helped to found and became the editor of the Russian religious-philosophical journal *Put'* (*The Path*), arguably the most important Russian religious journal ever published. He organized interconfessional meetings of representatives of Catholic, Protestant, and Orthodox religious-philosophical thought, with the participation of such figures as Maritain, Mounier, Marcel, and Barth.

In the émigré period, his thought was primarily directed toward what can be called a liberation from ontologism. Emigration became for him an existential experience of "rootless" extra-hierarchical existence, which can find a foundation solely in "the kingdom of the Spirit," i.e., in the person or personality. The primacy of "freedom" over "being" became the determining principle of his philosophy, a principle which found profound expression in his book *On the Destiny of Man: An Essay on Paradoxical Ethics* (1931), which he considered his "most perfect" book. This is how he expressed this principle: "creativeness is possible only if one admits freedom that is not determined by being, that is not derivable from being. Freedom is rooted not in being but in 'nothingness'; freedom is foundationless, is not determined by anything, is found outside of causal relations, to which being is subject and without which being cannot be understood" (from his autobiography, the Russian version, *Self-knowledge*, p. 231).

At around the same time, Berdyaev re-evaluated Kant's philosophy, arriving at the conclusion that only this philosophy "contains the foundations of a true metaphysics." In particular, Kant's "recognition that there is a deeper reality hidden behind the world of phenomena" helped Berdyaev formulate a key principle of his personalism: the doctrine of "objectification," which he first systematically developed in *The World of Objects: An Essay on the Philosophy of Solitude and Social Intercourse* (1934) (English title: *Solitude and Society*). This is how Berdyaev explained this doctrine: "Objectification is an epistemological interpretation of the fallenness of the world, of the state of enslavement, necessity, and disunitedness in which the world finds itself. The objectified world is subject to rational knowledge in concepts, but the objectification itself has an irrational source" (*Self-knowledge*, p. 292). Using man's creative powers, it is possible to pierce this layer of objectification, and to see the deeper reality. Man's "ego" (which knows only the objectified world) then regains its status of "person," which lives in the non-objectified, or real, world. Berdyaev had a strong sense of the unreality of the world around him, of his belonging to another—real—world.

After the Second World War, Berdyaev's reflections turned again to the role of Russia in the world. His first post-war book was *The Russian Idea: The Fundamental Problems of Russian Thought of the 19th Century and the Beginning of the 20th Century* (1946), in which he tried to discover the profound meaning of Russian thought and culture. Himself being one of the greatest representatives of this thought and culture, he saw that the meaning of his own activity was to reveal to the western world the distinctive elements of Russian philosophy, such as its existential nature, its eschatalogism, its religious anarchism, and its obsession with the idea of "Divine humanity."

Berdyaev is one of the greatest religious existentialists. His philosophy goes beyond mere thinking, mere rational conceptualization, and tries to attain authentic life itself: the profound layers of existence that touch upon God's world. He directed all of his efforts, philosophical as well as in his personal and public life, at replacing the kingdom of this world with the kingdom of God. According to him, we can all attempt to do this by tapping the divine creative powers which constitute our true nature. Our mission is to be collaborators with God in His continuing creation of the world.

Summing up his thought in one sentence, this is what Berdyaev said about himself: "Man, personality, freedom, creativeness, the eschatological-messianic resolution of the dualism of two worlds—these are my basic themes."

BORIS JAKIM

2009

BIBLIOGRAPHY OF NIKOLAI BERDYAEV'S
BOOKS IN ENGLISH TRANSLATION
(IN ALPHABETICAL ORDER)

The Beginning and the End. Russian edition 1947. First English edition 1952.

The Bourgeois Mind and Other Essays. English edition 1934.

Christian Existentialism. A Berdyaev Anthology. 1965.

Christianity and Anti-Semitism. Russian edition 1938. First English edition 1952.

Christianity and Class War. Russian edition 1931. First English edition 1933.

The Destiny of Man. Russian edition 1931. First English edition 1937.

The Divine and the Human. Russian edition 1952. First English edition 1947.

Dostoevsky: An Interpretation. Russian edition 1923. First English edition 1934.

Dream and Reality: An Essay in Autobiography. Russian edition 1949. First English edition 1950.

The End of Our Time. Russian edition 1924. First English edition 1933.

The Fate of Man in the Modern World. First Russian edition 1934. English edition 1935.

Freedom and the Spirit. Russian edition 1927. First English edition 1935.

Leontiev. Russian edition 1926. First English edition 1940.

The Meaning of History. Russian edition 1923. First English edition 1936.

The Meaning of the Creative Act. Russian edition 1916. First English edition 1955.

The Origin of Russian Communism. Russian edition 1937. First English edition 1937.

The Realm of Spirit and the Realm of Caesar. Russian edition 1949. First English edition 1952.

The Russian Idea. Russian edition 1946. First English edition 1947.

Slavery and Freedom. Russian edition 1939. First English edition 1939.

Solitude and Society. Russian edition 1934. First English edition 1938.

Spirit and Reality. Russian edition 1946. First English edition 1937.

Towards a New Epoch. Transl. from the original French edition 1949.

Truth and Revelation. English edition 1954.

[160]

www.ingramcontent.com/pod-product-compliance
Lightning Source LLC
Chambersburg PA
CBHW020333100426

42812CB00029B/3112/J